The Essential Guide for Student-Centered Coaching

Dedicated to our kids:
Quinn and Eva
Lorenzo, Lila, and Fiona

The Essential Guide for Student-Centered Coaching

What Every K–12 Coach and School Leader Needs to Know

Diane Sweeney
Leanna S. Harris

FOR INFORMATION:

Corwin

A SAGE Company

2455 Teller Road

Thousand Oaks, California 91320

(800) 233-9936

www.corwin.com

SAGE Publications Ltd.

1 Oliver's Yard

55 City Road

London EC1Y 1SP

United Kingdom

SAGE Publications India Pvt. Ltd.

B 1/I 1 Mohan Cooperative Industrial Area

Mathura Road, New Delhi 110 044

India

SAGE Publications Asia-Pacific Pte. Ltd.

18 Cross Street #10-10/11/12

China Square Central

Singapore 048423

Program Director and Publisher: Dan Alpert

Senior Content
   Development Editor: Lucas Schleicher

Associate Content
   Development Editor: Mia Rodriguez

Project Editor: Amy Schroller

Copy Editor: Megan Markanich

Typesetter: C&M Digitals (P) Ltd.

Proofreader: Lawrence W. Baker

Indexer: Wendy Allex

Cover Designer: Scott Van Atta

Marketing Manager: Maura Sullivan

Printed in the United States of America

Library of Congress Cataloging-in-Publication Data

Names: Sweeney, Diane, author. | Harris, Leanna S., author.

Title: The essential guide for student-centered coaching : what every K-12 coach and school leader needs to know / Diane Sweeney, Diane Sweeney Consulting, Denver, CO, Leanna S. Harris, Diane Sweeney Consulting, Denver, CO.

Description: Thousand Oaks, California : Corwin, [2020] | Includes bibliographical references and index.

Identifiers: LCCN 2019052361 | ISBN 9781544375359 (paperback) | ISBN 9781544394312 (epub) | ISBN 9781544394329 (epub) | ISBN 9781544394336 (pdf)

Subjects: LCSH: Student-centered learning—United States. | Educational leadership—United States. | Mentoring in education—United States.

Classification: LCC LB1027.23 .S94 2020 | DDC 371.39/4—dc23
LC record available at https://lccn.loc.gov/2019052361

This book is printed on acid-free paper.

23 24 10 9 8

Contents

Chapter 3. Understanding Our Impact   45

Chapter 4. Student-Centered Coaching Conversations   63

Chapter 5. Building a Culture Where Student-Centered Coaching Thrives   81

Visit the companion website at
Resources.corwin.com/EssentialGuideforSCCoaching
for downloadable resources.

List of Figures

Acknowledgments

Almost a decade after Diane launched the idea of Student-Centered Coaching, neither of us could imagine that things would come this far. What started with a simple question of "What about the kids?" has resulted in thousands of coaches, principals, and district administrators creating systems of professional learning for teachers that put student learning front and center.

Across the United States and beyond, in districts large and small, amazing coaching is happening. As we have the opportunity to work with coaches and administrators doing this important work, we are continually learning from their experiences. So it is only fitting that first and foremost we want to thank the coaches and leaders who have helped us refine and grow our thinking around Student-Centered Coaching. Your successes, adaptations, and challenges are woven into every part of this book.

We'd also like to thank the teachers who we've partnered with over the years. Their dedication, care, and concern for the students in their classrooms make coaching a true joy. There is no place we'd rather be than working alongside you in your classrooms.

We are also fortunate to work with an incredible team. Amanda Brueggeman, Joy Casey, Rachel Jenner, Ann Mausbach, Brooke O'Drobinak, Julie Steele, Karen Taylor, and Julie Wright are dedicated and passionate coaches/consultants whose experience and expertise continues to push this work forward in new ways. Heartfelt thanks go to each and every one of you.

Lastly, we'd like to thank both of our "Dans." Dan Alpert has been our thinking partner and editor since the publication of the first book on

Student-Centered Coaching. He has not only supported the work but asked us tough questions to make it better. And Dan Sweeney, our project manager and Diane's husband, clears the way so we can focus on what matters most. Thank you for all you do behind the scenes.

We aren't sure where this journey will take us next, but we are excited to find out. We hope you'll join us.

About the Authors

Diane Sweeney is the co-author of *Leading Student-Centered Coaching: Building Principal and Coach Partnerships* (Sweeney & Mausbach, 2018), *Student-Centered Coaching: The Moves* (Sweeney & Harris, 2017), and author of *Student-Centered Coaching: A Guide for K–8 Coaches and Principals* (2011), and *Student-Centered Coaching at the Secondary Level* (2013). Each of these books is grounded in the simple but powerful premise that coaching can be designed to more directly impact student learning. Her first book, *Learning Along the Way* (2003), shares the story of how an urban elementary school transformed itself to become a learning community.

Diane spends her time speaking and consulting for schools and educational organizations across the country. She is also an instructor for the University of Wisconsin–Madison. When she isn't working in schools, she loves to spend time outside with her family in Denver, Colorado.

Leanna S. Harris is the co-author of *Student-Centered Coaching: The Moves* (Sweeney & Harris, 2017). She has worked as a teacher, coach, and consultant across Grades K–12 and currently works with Diane Sweeney Consulting to help schools and districts implement Student-Centered Coaching. Her work is based upon the belief that professional development for teachers is most effective when it is grounded in outcomes for student achievement—for every child, every day.

Leanna is a passionate skier and cyclist. She lives in Denver, Colorado, with her husband and three kids.

Introduction

Student-Centered Coaching: A Guide for K–8 Coaches and Principals (Sweeney) was first published in 2011. It was the result of us wondering how to ensure that coaching makes a measurable impact on teaching and learning. Almost ten years later, we hope that we've helped schools and districts answer this question.

Nearly every conversation we have about coaching reminds us of how complex, challenging, and messy it really is. It sure would be nice if we could get around that fact, but working in the field of instructional coaching for over twenty years has taught us to embrace this reality. After all, most innovation is derived from problem solving, and the problem we seek to solve is how to continue to get more out of instructional coaching.

As you read this book, you'll notice that we present a close-up view of this important work. That's because we love to be right near the action. All year long we work alongside coaches, teachers, students, and their principals to help them develop the skills and strategies that are necessary to pull this off. We believe that taking a practitioner stance allows us to learn from, and make meaning of, the work. The icing on the cake is that we then get to share what we learn with others. Like you.

Why This Book Now?

A lot has changed in education over the past decade. New standards and curriculum were adopted, the Visible Learning research has become a driving force in understanding evidence-based instructional practice, and more school districts are investing in instructional coaching. It feels like now is the time to share our newest thinking about coaching.

We view this book as the essential guide for all things Student-Centered Coaching and therefore feel it has something for everyone. Those who are new to Student-Centered Coaching will find the foundational beliefs and practices for the work. Those who are familiar with Student-Centered Coaching will find a lot that's new. Our goal is to provide a belief system and a look at the practices we use as well as to address aspects of the work that we haven't discussed in our other books. This includes a framework for coaching cycles, how we engage in conversations that are student-centered, insights around building a culture for coaching, and methods for supporting and evaluating coaches.

We've designed this book to accompany *Student-Centered Coaching: The Moves* (Sweeney & Harris, 2017) and *Leading Student-Centered Coaching: Building Principal and Coach Partnerships* (Sweeney & Mausbach, 2018). *Student-Centered Coaching: The Moves* serves as a how-to book and is chock-full of tools, strategies, and videos of coaching in action. It answers the question, "What does Student-Centered Coaching look like in practice?" *Leading Student-Centered Coaching* addresses the importance of building principal and coach partnerships that are aligned with school improvement processes. Without these partnerships, the impact of coaching will be diminished. Our hope is that together these books will build a comprehensive view of how to implement Student-Centered Coaching in your school or district.

Guiding Principles and Core Practices

Whenever we are working with others to implement Student-Centered Coaching, we continually come back to a set of guiding principles that serve as the philosophical underpinning for this work. These principles are at the heart of our beliefs about coaching as well as our practices, and they hold us accountable to staying "student-centered" in everything we do.

- Coaching is not about "fixing" teachers.
- Coaching is a partnership focused on student learning.
- Coaching is about continual professional growth.
- Coaching is part of a robust ecosystem of professional learning.

In addition to our guiding principles, we use seven core practices for Student-Centered Coaching. Each one is rooted in the teaching and learning cycle, and together, they address the process of a coaching cycle as well as the importance of measuring the impact of coaching and partnering with school leadership. The core practices for Student-Centered Coaching are as follows, and they are described in more detail in Figure 1.3 in Chapter 1.

1. Utilize coaching cycles

2. Set standards-based goals

3. Unpack the goal into learning targets

4. Co-plan with student evidence

5. Co-teach using effective instructional practices

6. Measure the impact on student and teacher learning

7. Partner with the leader

The Path to Implementation of Student-Centered Coaching

As we mentioned, coaching is messy. We've learned this in our work with schools and districts across the United States and beyond. As you either think about or intentionally move toward implementation, this is a road map to follow. It doesn't mean that there won't be detours, breakdowns, or other challenges. But it does provide you with a path to make your goals for instructional coaching a reality.

The stages of implementation include prelaunch; launch; and implement, monitor, and adjust. The duration of each stage is based on the needs of the district or organization. Here is a description of the roles played by the district, school principal, and coach in each stage of implementation:

DISTRICT—Builds stakeholders' knowledge of the purpose and practices for Student-Centered Coaching. Hires a well-qualified coaching team.

PRINCIPAL—Studies the purpose and practices for Student-Centered Coaching in order to lead the effort with clarity of purpose.

COACH—Studies the purpose and practices for Student-Centered Coaching. Builds trusting and respectful relationships with teachers.

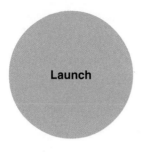

DISTRICT—Provides professional learning to the coaching team. Works with school leaders to implement Student-Centered Coaching.

PRINCIPAL—Aligns coaching with the school improvement plan. Introduces coaching to the faculty, clarifying what coaching is and isn't and addressing questions or concerns among teachers.

COACH—Partners with the principal to launch coaching cycles. Develops systems for collecting evidence of impact.

DISTRICT—Collects district-level data to monitor the impact of the coaching program. Continues to provide professional learning to the coaching team and principals.

PRINCIPAL—Meets with the coach on a weekly basis. Continues to monitor the impact of coaching in relation to the school improvement plan.

COACH—Continues to implement coaching cycles and collect evidence of impact. Collaborates with the principal to maintain focus and develop coaching skills.

Coaching is a journey that we have been on for many years now. In the pages of this book you will learn about the countless mistakes we've made and lessons we've learned. As you embark upon or continue your own journey with coaching, we hope this essential guide will provide you with insights, ideas, and inspiration.

Why Student-Centered Coaching Matters

1

We had a wake-up call early in our coaching work. A school on the Navajo reservation in southeastern Utah had invited us to work with their teachers on the instruction of reading comprehension. To get there, we flew ninety minutes on a sixteen-seat plane and then drove across the desert to arrive in the town of Mexican Hat. If you've ever seen the film *Thelma & Louise*, you've seen this beautiful part of the country.

On our first visit, the principal shared some assessment data that indicated that many students were performing below grade level in reading. He then led us on a tour to meet the teachers who we would be working with. As less-than-experienced coaches, we didn't think to ask how this list of teachers had been created or how they felt about being on it. Instead, we took it as our cue to go from classroom to classroom to show the teachers how it's done. We thought that if on each visit we planned, modeled, and debriefed lessons, then the teachers would continue using the practices after we left. To put it simply, we were taking a "show-and-tell" approach to professional development. We would *show* the teachers what teaching reading looked like, and we would *tell* them how they could do it. Then we'd fly home making the assumption that it would somehow make a difference for their students.

As we arrived at the school for a visit in the early spring, we learned that all of the teachers we were scheduled to work with had called in sick. Since no other teachers were ill that day, it suddenly became obvious that the problem was us. We had to face the hard reality that what we were doing wasn't working. Looking back, it's easy to see what led us astray. We thought that our role was to support teachers to implement a specific set of instructional practices, and we tackled this by showing teachers how to teach. To the teachers it must have felt very top down, bossy, and condescending. It's no wonder they called in sick.

Experiences like this helped us shift toward our current approach to coaching. It was clear that downloading instructional strategies onto the teachers was a rookie mistake—one that we learned from the hard way.

We Don't Have Time to Waste

Our students don't go to school to participate in programs, they don't go to school to behave, and they don't go to school to score well on tests. They go to school to learn, so it only makes sense that this should be the focus of our coaching. If our ultimate goal is to increase student achievement, then coaching should be designed to do just that.

There is no shortage of school districts that are looking for more from their coaching programs. The question is how to get there. Many have had coaches without a clear plan for coaching. In these cases, nobody really knows what to expect from working with a coach. This includes teachers, school leaders, and even the coaches themselves.

It's no surprise that so many educators aren't clear about what coaching is about. In a recent review of research on instructional coaching, we were struck by how often it is described as being about improving instructional practice to ultimately impact student achievement. Teachers may wonder what this really means in their day-to-day life with students, and they may even assume that coaching is about determining what they're doing wrong and how the coach is going to "fix" them. Clearly this was the impression shared by the teachers in Mexican Hat.

This vision of coaching also implies that changing instruction will *hopefully* trickle down to improving student learning, but how would we know for sure? There is a clear argument to be made for having a highly effective teacher in every classroom (Darling-Hammond, Hyler, & Gardner, 2017). Yet when coaching focuses solely on improving instruction, the focus is on implementing a certain practice, strategy, or structure. When this is the case it's easy to lose sight of the real goal, which is student learning.

Student-Centered Coaching takes a different approach. Rather than just *hoping* that coaching will impact student learning, this is our focus. We ask teachers what they would like their students to learn, and then co-plan and co-teach to get them there. In this way we not only impact student learning but we also support teachers to implement effective instructional practices along the way. This is because we co-plan lessons that are rich with the research-based instructional practices that we hope to see. This creates buy-in and relevance among teachers while also building their pedagogical skills. We don't have the luxury of focusing our coaching on instruction in isolation and then hoping that student learning will follow suit. We must design our coaching in a way that is aimed at a concrete goal for student learning and then partner with teachers on the instructional practices that will get us there.

Built on a Philosophy of Backward Design

When we were grappling with how to be more effective in our coaching, we were also studying *Understanding by Design* by Wiggins and McTighe (2005). It came together when we read, "We ask designers to start with a much more careful statement of the desired results—the priority *learnings*—and to derive the curriculum from the performances called for or implied in the goals" (p. 17). This notion of working backward from the desired results became the operating principle for Student-Centered Coaching.

With the focus on a goal for student learning, it became easier to develop partnerships with teachers. Even more importantly, the impact became measurable because the teacher and coach could formatively assess student learning every step of the way. We were also able to identify the growth that the teacher had made instructionally because it was nested in the context of teaching *and* learning.

How Student-Centered Coaching Compares With Other Approaches to Coaching

Figure 1.1 compares Student-Centered Coaching with other approaches to instructional coaching. While you may have seen a similar figure in our previous publications, we've updated it with the hope of showing how coaching can get us closer to student learning right off the bat. You'll notice that we use the language of relationship-driven, teacher-centered, and student-centered coaching in order to describe what we've seen in schools as we've supported coaching over the past few decades. This figure describes the role, focus, use of data, and other common coaching behaviors in each type of coaching.

FIGURE 1.1   Student-Centered, Teacher-Centered, and Relationship-Driven Coaching

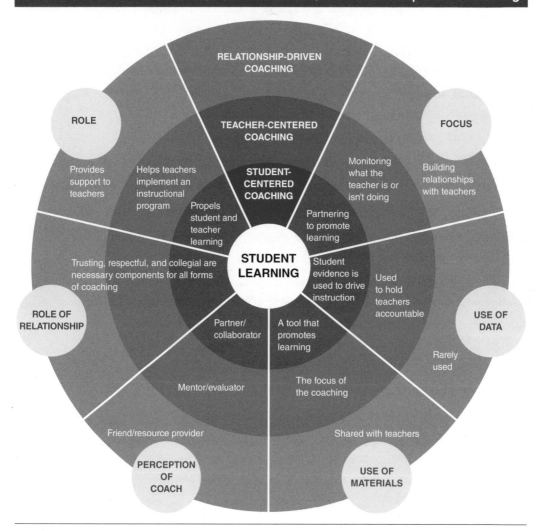

We like to think of this figure as a dartboard. When playing darts, we aim for the bullseye at the center. In this case, the center is student learning. The closer our darts are to the bullseye, the bigger our impact is on student learning. While it would be nice if we hit the center every time, we know that there are times when we may hit the outer rings. From time to time, we may serve as a resource provider or engage in some teacher-centered coaching because we are striving to be responsive to the teachers' needs. However, if we are hitting the outer rings all of the time, or if our role is defined as relationship-driven or teacher-centered coaching, then we will make far less of an impact on student learning. The objective of Student-Centered Coaching is to be aiming for the bullseye as much as possible.

Teacher Perception Matters

Understanding teacher perception is essential if we hope to successfully implement a coaching effort. The reason for this is simple: teacher perception connects directly to buy-in, trust, and willingness to engage wholeheartedly in coaching.

Teacher-centered coaching is the most challenging place to build trusting relationships with teachers. When coaches are put in the position of monitoring whether or not teachers are implementing the program or practices, they become closely affiliated with accountability. This is the role we took in our work with the teachers in Mexican Hat. They most likely viewed us as coming in and telling them what to do, which negatively impacted their perception of coaching.

Relationship-driven coaching can also negatively impact how teachers view coaching. The reason for this is it can feel unfocused or like it's a waste of time. In other words, coaching may not be taken seriously because teachers don't have time for things that are not laser-like focused on their students' achievement.

Unlike these other approaches to coaching, Student-Centered Coaching emphasizes the use of student evidence to propel student and teacher learning forward. Taking this stance leads to the perception that coaching is not only worth a teacher's time but it is beneficial to the students as well. This enables us to create partnerships far more quickly.

As you read through the different approaches to coaching, you've probably begun to reflect on what coaching looks like in your school or district. For example, do teachers see the coach merely as a resource provider? Do they steer clear of coaching because they see it as not fitting their needs? Or are they engaged because they understand the value it brings to their students' learning? Figure 1.2 provides a series of questions to gauge how coaching is perceived by the teachers in your school.

The good news is it's never too late to shift in the direction of Student-Centered Coaching—especially when we engage teachers in the process. Time and time again, we see them valuing coaching when they understand that it's about their students' learning because that's what matters most.

FIGURE 1.2 Reflecting on Teacher Perception

1. If we were to ask teachers in your school why coaching matters, what would they say?

2. What do you think has led to this perception?

3. Do coaches feel that building relationships is their ultimate goal, or is relationship-building viewed as a first step for coaching?

4. How much time do coaches spend gathering and providing resources to teachers? In what ways is this impacting how they are perceived by teachers?

5. Are coaches engaged in work that is solely focused on implementation of specific instructional practices, or is their work learning focused?

6. Are there ways to survey teachers to better understand their perceptions about coaching?

Core Practices for Student-Centered Coaching

Coaches often wonder what effective coaching looks like. Student-Centered Coaching is driven by seven core practices that are all about keeping student learning at the center of each and every conversation. This is how we ensure that we stay at the center of the bullseye. The core practices are illustrated in Figure 1.3. For more information on how to put them into action, we'd recommend our companion book, *Student-Centered Coaching: The Moves* (Sweeney & Harris, 2017).

FIGURE 1.3 Core Practices for Student-Centered Coaching

CORE PRACTICE	PURPOSE
1. Utilize coaching cycles	Coaching cycles create the conditions for a coach to make a lasting impact. If coaches work with teachers in an informal, or one-shot, basis, then the results of coaching will be diminished.
2. Set standards-based goals	We frame coaching around student learning by setting standards-based goals for coaching cycles. This not only helps teachers see the value in coaching but it also helps us ensure that we are setting high expectations for all students.
3. Unpack the goal into learning targets	Student-friendly learning targets increase instructional clarity. They serve as a success criteria for the coaching cycle and provide a mechanism for formative assessment by the teacher and self-assessment by the students.

CORE PRACTICE	PURPOSE
4. Co-plan with student evidence	Student evidence is used to drive decision-making when planning lessons. This aligns with our belief that coaching is built on a foundation of formative assessment.
5. Co-teach using effective instructional practices	Rather than modeling or observing, we advocate for coaches and teachers to build partnerships while working together in the classroom. This includes using a variety of coaching moves that increase teacher metacognition and transfer of practice.
6. Measure the impact on student and teacher learning	It is our obligation to collect data to demonstrate how teachers and students are growing across coaching cycles. Using the Results-Based Coaching Tool (RBCT) provides a way to clearly articulate our impact.
7. Partner with the school leader	Without a solid principal and coach partnership, the coach will not be able to make the desired impact. Clearly defining roles, separating coaching from evaluation, and creating systems for principal and coach collaboration build a culture for coaching.

Creating an Ecosystem for Professional Learning and Coaching

Successful coaching programs are embedded into what we like to refer to as an ecosystem for professional learning. The definition of an ecosystem is a complex network or interconnected system, which we feel expresses the kind of aligned and connected system that schools need to have for meaningful learning to take place.

When we think of coaching as an essential component of the broader system for teacher development, we avoid positioning it as one more thing that teachers have to do, but rather as something that is embedded into the existing school improvement processes (Sweeney & Mausbach, 2018). Figure 1.4 unpacks this further by demonstrating how coaching and professional learning work together to impact student and teacher learning.

You'll notice that we use the language of "the thing" to define a high-leverage strategy as the focus for school improvement—for example, implementing balanced literacy, using strategies for disciplinary literacy, building teacher clarity, or using ongoing formative assessment. The key is for "the thing" to be focused.

It's paramount to have teachers' voices in the conversation when it comes to identifying "the thing." Asking what they are experiencing in the

FIGURE 1.4   How Coaching Connects to Existing Structures for Professional Learning

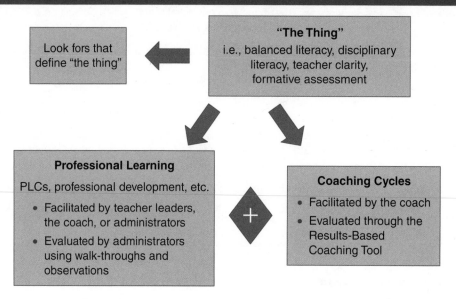

Source: Adapted from Sweeney & Mausbach (2018).

classroom and what they think matters most goes a long way in building a culture of learning. We even find ourselves referring to "the thing" as "the dream" because it is something that is good for the students and is agreed upon by the teachers.

Establishing Look Fors

After a focus has been identified, it's important to unpack it into a set of look fors so we can become clear about what we mean when we claim it as our focus for school improvement. Well-crafted look fors provide the specificity that the administration needs to monitor implementation. When a principal walks into a classroom with a set of look fors, the likelihood of quality feedback increases. When look fors are lacking, it is much harder for the principal to supervise and for the coach to provide support. Figure 1.5 provides an example of look fors from a middle school that was focusing on increasing teacher clarity to increase self-regulation by students.

Professional Learning

After a focus (or "the thing") and look fors have been identified, it's time to consider how the teachers will be supported. We offer two ways to

FIGURE 1.5   Examples of Look Fors

"THE THING": INCREASING TEACHER CLARITY TO INCREASE SELF-REGULATION BY STUDENTS

Look Fors

- Teachers will embed student-friendly learning targets into each lesson.
- Students will self-assess in relation to the learning targets at least one time per lesson.
- When asked, students will be able to articulate the purpose for learning.
- Students will be grouped flexibly and in relation to the learning targets.
- Conferences with students will be guided by the learning targets.

achieve this: professional learning and coaching cycles. Both are equally important. Professional learning includes collaboration through PLCs, learning teams, department meetings, data teams, and more traditional forms of professional development. Coaching cycles occur one-on-one, with pairs, or small groups, and they provide the opportunity for a coach to guide teachers toward implementation within their classrooms.

We recommend for professional learning to be facilitated by a broad array of leaders including teacher leaders, the coach, or the principal because this creates a culture of learning that integrates voices from across the faculty. A simple way to accomplish this is to create a leadership team that plans and delivers professional learning that relates to the focus for school improvement. For example, teachers can lead PLCs, they can provide professional learning, and they can even open up their classrooms for peer-based observations. Including a variety of voices in this conversation helps us avoid delegating professional learning to the coach, a move that doesn't acknowledge the voices, ideas, or strengths of the teachers in the school.

With a clear focus on school improvement comes the need for monitoring and supervision by the school leader. When walk-throughs are focused and include quality feedback, they can be one of the best ways to ensure that teachers are successfully implementing what is expected. By quality feedback, we mean to suggest that whenever principals spend time in a classroom, they circle back with the teacher to discuss how the teaching and learning aligned with the look fors and what might come next.

When it comes to monitoring and supervision, we keep the coaches out of it. This means they aren't engaging in walk-throughs or other forms of evaluation. Rather, they are rolling up their sleeves and supporting teachers through coaching cycles.

Coaching Cycles

Coaching cycles sit alongside professional learning and serve a different purpose. They are driven by a standards-based goal that is identified by the teachers who are involved, and they include regular co-planning and co-teaching sessions with the coach. While it is far more subtle, the look fors are a part of coaching cycles through embedded classroom-based work. For example, a coach working in a school focused on teacher clarity will find plenty of opportunities to integrate the look fors into co-planning and co-teaching sessions by asking questions such as the following: (1) What will our learning target be for the lesson? (2) What strategies do we want students to use to self-assess? (3) How will we organize small groups?

Rather than downloading information onto teachers about every-thing they should be doing, the coach is able to integrate it right into the planning conversations. This approach keeps the coach away from accountability while staying firmly in the role of partner and support in implementing the given practices.

Where school leaders monitor the impact of professional learning through processes like walk-throughs, coaches monitor the impact of coaching cycles using a tool we refer to as the Results-Based Coaching Tool (RBCT). This allows coaches to walk away from coaching cycles, understanding how both the teacher and students grew.

Chapter 2 provides more information about how to organize and facilitate coaching cycles, and for more on aligning coaching with school improve-ment processes, refer to *Leading Student-Centered Coaching: Building Principal and Coach Partnerships* (Sweeney & Mausbach, 2018).

Coaching Toward Sustainability

We often hear the question, "How can we be sure that teachers will con-tinue to use the instructional practices after the cycle ends?" It's a fair question considering the number of resources that are put into having coaches in a school or district. None of us want coaching to feel like the movie *Groundhog Day*; waking up and not seeing a bit of progress is clearly not what we are looking for. We experienced this when working on the Navajo reservation. Not only did the teachers avoid us but they avoided the strategies we discussed as well. What a waste of time, energy, and resources.

While we strive to see shifts in instructional practice, this question can sometimes feel loaded, as though it's the coach's job to monitor implementation. This takes coaching in an evaluative direction, which is the last place we want to be. When coaches find that the work they're doing in coaching cycles doesn't result in any changes in teaching practice, it can be a good opportunity for reflection, just as we had to do all those years ago. We can ask ourselves questions such as these:

- *Did I keep the teacher in the driver's seat, or was I coaching to my own agenda?*

- *Did I do too much of the work, taking away the learning opportunity for the teacher?*

- *Did I overwhelm the teacher with too many of my own ideas?*

- *Did I create a system that allowed for consistent co-planning and co-teaching toward a goal for student learning, or was our work haphazard and unfocused?*

We can agree that whatever we do as coaches must be sustainable. The sentiment should be that anything we do in a coaching cycle should be something that the teacher can do on his or her own once the cycle is over. This happens when the coach acts as a partner in the process rather than as a resource with short-term fixes and supports. The following strategies are designed to not only increase the level of sustainability but to increase teacher ownership as well.

Guide Teachers Toward Work That Matters

A lesson in human behavior is that we won't work hard unless we care about the work. Finding things that teachers care about begins with the goal-setting conversation. When a coach asks, "What do you want your students to know and do?" we increase teacher ownership because teachers inherently want their students to be successful. Tapping into this powerful energy source is the engine that drives Student-Centered Coaching.

We like to borrow from the work of McTighe and Wiggins (2012), who refer to this as transfer of learning, or "the idea that engaging learners in thoughtful meaning making helps them deepen their understanding of important ideas and processes" (p. 3). This notion of transfer applies to teachers because we want what was learned to become embedded into daily practice.

One way we achieve this is to create meaningful work for both the students and teacher. We believe that meaningful work begins with framing coaching around a goal for student learning. This seems so obvious, but in our experience, it's still not common practice. Many coaching conversations focus on everything except learning—for example, how well a lesson is paced, if classroom management strategies are being used, or if the content is being covered. In contrast, if we organize coaching around a standards-based goal that the teacher cares about, then we are able to create transfer, and transfer ensures sustainability.

Take a Strengths-Based Approach With Adult Learners

While we know to avoid taking a deficit perspective toward students, why do we so often go there with teachers? It can happen in the subtlest of ways. A principal notices that behavior issues are escalating in a certain classroom, so we'd better get that teacher some coaching. Teachers are complaining that their students aren't coming to them prepared from the previous grade level. Again, let's get those teachers some coaching. Or test data is raising concerns regarding student growth and achievement. You guessed it! That teacher needs coaching.

Applying coaching through a deficit lens quickly becomes an uphill battle. Teachers figure out that coaching is about fixing them. They may feel as though they are being unfairly judged. They may resist due to feeling defensive. Or they may engage in ways that are inauthentic and have no intention of following through on anything that is discussed during the coaching sessions. This obviously goes against building sustainability.

This doesn't mean that building on strengths is a touchy-feely endeavor. Rather, it is a way to honor the work and knowledge that each teacher brings—before we make any adjustments. We will dig deeper into taking a strengths-based approach in Chapter 4.

Connections to the Visible Learning Research

How many times have you wondered if a certain strategy or instructional practice was as effective as you hoped it would be? The good news is we have a research base to guide our decision-making as educators. *Visible Learning* was introduced by John Hattie in his groundbreaking research that was first published in 2009. As of 2019, Hattie has analyzed more than 95,000 studies, 300 million students, and 250+ influences to understand what most influences student achievement. Hattie and Zierer (2018) write, "The aim is to move from 'what works' to 'what works best' and when, for whom, and why" (p. xviii).

Visible Learning is based on the idea that our responsibility as educators is to "know thy impact." Otherwise we may be using practices, programs, or interventions that aren't working for our students. Student-Centered Coaching operates from the same premise. By never wavering to monitor our impact, we maintain a disciplined focus on how a coach and teacher are (or aren't) moving student learning forward. Then we work together to figure out where to go next.

Figure 1.6 provides a crosswalk between the practices for Student-Centered Coaching and some of the influences that have been identified in the Visible Learning research. Each Visible Learning influence includes an effect size. Effect size is a common calculation that is used in the field of educational research as it allows us to place a large number of studies and amount of meta-analysis on a common scale.

As you explore the figure, you'll notice that the influences we've identified have an effect size of greater than $d = 0.40$. This is because $d = 0.40$ is considered the "hinge point," meaning that $d = 0.40$ equates to one year's growth in learning in one year's time. For a frame of reference, the highest effect size to date is collective teacher efficacy at 1.39, and an example of a low effect size is student retention at -0.32.

Let's take a closer look at how some of these influences align with Student-Centered Coaching, beginning with the largest effect size to date: collective teacher efficacy ($d = 1.39$). Donohoo (2018) writes, "When

FIGURE 1.6	How Student-Centered Coaching Aligns With the Visible Learning Research

STUDENT-CENTERED COACHING	VISIBLE LEARNING INFLUENCES	EFFECT SIZE
Partner with teachers to achieve standards mastery	– Collective teacher efficacy	$d = 1.39$
	– Mastery learning	$d = 0.61$
	– Teacher expectations	$d = 0.43$
Co-plan and co-teach with teachers	– Clear goal intentions	$d = 0.48$
	– Teacher clarity	$d = 0.75$
	– Metacognitive strategies	$d = 0.69$
Use formative assessment practices	– Evaluation and reflection	$d = 0.75$
	– Self-regulation strategies	$d = 0.52$
	– Evaluation and reflection	$d = 0.75$
Support student engagement through quality work	– Strong classroom cohesion	$d = 0.53$
	– Classroom management	$d = 0.52$
	– Teacher-student relationship	$d = 0.48$

Source: Author created using data from Hattie (2019, June). Retrieved from https://us.corwin.com/sites/default/files/250_influences_chart_june_2019.pdf.

teachers believe that together they and their colleagues can impact student achievement, they share a sense of collective teacher efficacy. Collective efficacy is high when teachers believe that the staff is capable of helping students master complex content, fostering students' creativity, and getting students to believe they can do well in school" (p. 3). One of the most important jobs for coaches is to help teachers believe that they can have a positive impact on their students. This means we work with teachers to create a path forward through having meaningful formative assessment, co-planning high-quality lessons, and creating an overall belief that students can get there when we work together to create the proper conditions for learning.

Collective teacher efficacy connects to another important influence, mastery learning ($d = 0.61$). By helping teachers envision how to better serve all students, coaches can break down the barriers associated with low teacher expectations. This, in turn, creates schools where students are provided with the instruction that they deserve. As coaches, we aren't satisfied until all learners have reached the goal for the coaching cycle. Sure, this may take some work, but if we don't maintain this mindset then we are making assumptions based on who we think should or shouldn't achieve. Teaching to mastery elevates expectations for all students, and it is rewarding and motivating when teachers experience this kind of success with their students.

By influencing what happens every day in the classroom, coaches and teachers design and execute lessons that are clearer to both the teacher and the students. This connects to the influence of teacher clarity ($d = 0.76$), which is almost twice the average effect size of one year of schooling. Almarode and Vandas (2018) describe teacher clarity as follows:

> When teachers are clear on what students are learning, they can better select learning experiences that specifically target the necessary learning. Similarly, when teachers know why students are learning what they are learning, they can better design learning experiences that are authentic and relevant to learners. Finally, when teachers know what success looks like, they can show learners what success looks like, design opportunities for students to make their own thinking and learning visible, give and receive feedback, and gather evidence about where to go next in the teaching and learning. (p. 5)

Because Student-Centered Coaching is designed to impact student learning, it guides teachers toward using practices that are research proven, most likely to increase student achievement, and aligned with the Visible Learning research.

Lesson From the Field

Heather had been teaching sixth-grade math for five years in a district north of Denver, Colorado. About 60 percent of the students in her school were from low-income families, and the population of nonnative English speakers had been growing rapidly each year due to a demographic shift in the neighborhood.

Due to low test scores, the district began pushing for an inquiry-based approach to mathematics. In theory, this sounded good to Heather, but somehow it just wasn't playing out in her classroom. She knew she was doing the bulk of the work during her math lessons—for example, explaining step-by-step how to do problems and then watching kids sit helplessly waiting for her to come assist them one by one during independent practice time. When she put the students into small groups to discuss their work, she found that they would either sit silently or chat about topics completely unrelated to math. She left each day feeling exhausted from all the hard work she was doing, and yet she knew deep down that her students weren't getting it. She was on a fast track to teacher burnout.

That same year, her principal launched a cohort with the math teachers and Joy, their newly hired instructional coach. They met twice a month to read and learn more about best practices for teaching math. The expectation was that they would try new things and report back on how it was going. A few of the teachers would come back with good news to report, but mostly the group expressed frustration from not feeling successful. Some lacked confidence in the whole process and refused to even try anything in the first place.

Heather implemented a few of the things they were learning, but mainly she saw the same results: kids not engaging in the work, giving up quickly because it was "too hard," and being off task when asked to work with their peers.

A few weeks later, they gathered in the conference room as usual, but this time the principal asked Joy to take the lead. "I've been practicing some new strategies for coaching," Joy said. "Along with continuing to learn alongside you in our study group, I'd like to partner with you as you work to implement this work in your classrooms." She went on to explain the philosophy of Student-Centered Coaching and how it would enable her to work side by side with the teachers as they endeavored to change how they were teaching math. Heather, desperate for *something* to help her make it through the rest of the year, decided to go for it.

The first thing Joy did when she met with Heather was to lay the foundation for their work together. She explained that they would focus on just one of Heather's sections. They would co-plan and co-teach for that class throughout the cycle. Together they chose some specific days and times to do this each week. Joy was sure to block these days off on her calendar to be certain that Heather would be her number one priority during those times. Then she made sure Heather understood that her purpose as a coach was to partner to help her students learn, *not* to teach and evaluate Heather on how to best teach math. They would set a goal for student learning, and everything they did would revolve around that goal.

Over the next six weeks, Heather and Joy did the work of teaching together. They set a goal for her third-period class: Students will understand and use ratios in order to make sense of real-world situations based on standards and their district math curriculum. They created a set of learning targets to guide their work with students, and they pre-assessed the students with an open-ended math task called the Ticket Booth Problem (see Figure 1.7).

Heather had never been much of a believer in pre-assessing because in the past when she'd given her students a bunch of problems to solve before she had taught them how to do the math, they mostly just left the whole thing blank. When Joy brought a more accessible and meaningful option to the table, Heather began to appreciate her as a resource. Not

---

FIGURE 1.7   Ticket Booth Problem From a Sixth-Grade Unit of Ratios and Proportions

A school carnival ticket booth posts the following sign:

TICKET BOOTH

1 Ticket For $.50

12 Tickets For $5.00

25 Tickets For $10.00

50 Tickets For $25.00

120 Tickets For $50.00

HAVE FUN !

1. Which number of tickets offers the best deal? Explain your thinking.
2. How would you suggest the students running the ticket booth modify the list of prices?

surprisingly, none of the students were able to demonstrate proficiency, but all of them were able to attempt to solve the problem, giving Heather and Joy valuable insight into what they were already bringing to the table as mathematicians.

As the pair began to co-plan and co-teach after collecting their baseline data, it was slow going for the first few weeks. Joy would persistently ask Heather questions during their planning. Mostly this was focused on helping the students think intentionally about what they needed to do: What is the specific learning target for this lesson? How will we unpack it to make sure kids know what's expected of them? What do they need at the beginning of the lesson to make sure they can be successful when working independently or in groups? What misconceptions might we expect to see? As they thought through all of these questions, they referred to the learning they'd been doing in their math cohort for guidance on how to make it all happen. Heather felt exhausted and overwhelmed at first, but the changes she was starting to see in her classroom gave her the energy to keep going.

Throughout the process, Joy worked hard to keep asking thoughtful questions and to help break down all the possibilities with Heather to be able to anticipate what would happen during the lesson. Most importantly, she kept the focus on the students and how they were doing toward meeting the goal. Heather felt this was key in making the process feel safe and supportive. Knowing that Joy would be with her on those set times each week kept her accountable to do what they said they would do, and at the same time it felt easier to take risks and try new things, knowing she was not going through it alone.

By the end of the coaching cycle, Heather was a different teacher, and her class was a different place. She was still working hard, but she was much more focused on *what* she was saying versus *how much* she was saying and doing for the kids. Her students were doing the bulk of the heavy lifting in class, including working with each other to struggle through hard problems, justifying their thinking, and persevering. Heather was taking all the great learning she did with Joy and applying it to her teaching and planning in her other sections. Across the board she was seeing great results, and for the first time in a long time she was enjoying teaching.

Tools and Techniques

While we've worked for years supporting the development of coaches, we've learned that they can't do it alone. In addition to having a skilled coach, Student-Centered Coaching requires a principal who understands the rationale and practices for this type of coaching and articulates with confidence how it positively impacts student learning. This process of articulation hinges on creating a plan for defining what Student-Centered Coaching means for both the teachers and students.

Being savvy regarding the messaging around coaching may feel like the principal is being asked to serve as a cheerleader for the work. It's a whole lot like marketing a product. Teachers have to believe in coaching, and if they sense even the smallest lack of support by the principal, then some may take that as an excuse to remain on the sidelines. The steps in Figure 1.8 walk us through how to build excitement around coaching. These are presented in an intentional order because starting with the *why* is how we begin to win the hearts and minds of teachers.

As we develop our own vision for coaching, a next step is to help others understand it as well. Let's not underestimate the fact that in most schools, coaching is either relationship driven or teacher-centered. For this reason, it may take some time to support teachers (and school leaders) to understand what it's all about. Figure 1.9 provides language to get us there.

FIGURE 1.8 Steps to Build Excitement Around Coaching

1. **Define why coaching matters**. *Articulate why teachers should care.*

2. **Communicate how coaching aligns with other district initiatives**. *Make sure teachers understand that coaching isn't one more thing.*

3. **Share the coach's role and how it folds into the plan for school improvement**. *Help teachers see the coach as inherent to the school's success.*

4. **Describe the expectations for teacher participation in coaching**. *Identify what participation looks like and how much time it will take.*

5. **Outline how teachers will be provided with choice and ownership in the coaching process**. *Make coaching about more than compliance.*

The if/then charts at the end of each chapter can also be found in Resource A in this book.

FIGURE 1.9 Language for Making a Shift to Student-Centered Coaching	
IF I HEAR . . .	**THEN I CAN USE THE FOLLOWING LANGUAGE . . .**
"I don't see any need to do a whole coaching cycle right now. Can you just help me with a few ideas for my upcoming unit?"	"I am happy to brainstorm some ideas with you, but I believe we can have a much bigger impact if we could partner throughout the whole unit. That way we can try different things along the way and make adjustments based on how the students are responding."
"I feel pretty good with the new math program, so I don't think you need to come in and give me any help with it."	"I'm glad to hear you're feeling good about the new program. My job as a coach is not to be the 'implementation enforcer' but rather to partner with teachers on their goals for student learning. What would you think about trying a coaching cycle with me to see how different this approach to coaching feels?"
A principal says, "I have some serious concerns about Mr. Seltzer's classroom management. With all of my other duties, I really need you to get in there and help him get on the right track."	"While I realize that you have some concerns, I wonder if we can take another approach to this. If I go in to work with Mr. Seltzer uninvited, I will be seen as a 'fixer,' which will undermine all the hard work we've done to create a positive culture around coaching. If you were to express your concerns to him and then suggest he seek out working with me for support, I think it will go a long way in keeping me away from the role of supervisor."

A Final Thought

This chapter makes the case for why Student-Centered Coaching matters. It also brings forth the level of intentionality that is required to implement a successful coaching program. No longer does coaching have to be something that teachers endure. No longer does it have to feel like a hammer that is there to ensure they are stepping in line.

Making this shift may be easier than you think. Will coaches need support from their principal and district? Sure. Will they need a clearly defined role? Definitely. And will they need to see the value in this work? Absolutely. With these pieces in place, it's never too late to make coaching about both student *and* teacher learning. Let's switch it up so that teachers clamor for, rather than avoid, this precious resource. We will always be reminded that this is messy work. We like to think of it as joyfully messy because the complexity of designing and implementing a coaching model is rich with opportunity, growth, and renewal.

Coaching Cycles

An Essential Practice

2

//

Having never played an instrument and truly knowing nothing about music, Leanna decided that learning to play the ukulele would provide a fun and worthy challenge. Her friend Blair graciously offered to loan her a ukulele along with a beginner's book to get her going. Excited, she brought it home in its little black case and set it by her favorite chair in the living room.

Three weeks later, the ukulele hadn't moved. Is it in tune? How do you hold it? What do those little diagrams in the book mean? Leanna just couldn't find a way to get started. She asked Blair if he would give her a rundown of the basics, and he walked her through a few things like hand position and tuning. Leanna cracked open the book and gave it a try. It was slow going, but she felt good to finally be starting. She practiced again the next day, and the one after that, but then her effort fizzled. Another few weeks went by before she checked out a "Learn to Play the Ukulele" video on YouTube and finally picked it up again. She put in a few good practice sessions, energized by the progress she was making, but after several days of this she hit another lull. She didn't know what her next steps should be, and there was always something more urgent she needed to be doing when it came time to practice. *I promise I'll practice tomorrow!* she thought.

After many more tomorrows, Leanna realized that what she was doing just wasn't working. She needed to be more focused and intentional if she really wanted to learn to play this instrument, so she enrolled in a class at a local music school. Each Monday night, Leanna joined eight other ukulele novices to practice strumming patterns and chord sequences as well as to get helpful feedback from her teacher. Knowing she would need to show up to the next class having made some progress, she committed to practice at least three times a week.

By the end of the eight-week class, her strumming was flowing, and the transition between chords was becoming more fluid. She could even play a few basic songs. Committing the time and resources to the class was just the push Leanna needed. When she was more intentional about her learning and had a reason to hold herself accountable, she was more motivated to practice, she benefited from the feedback, and her learning soared.

Trying to get better at something is hard to do in isolation and without structure. It's challenging to commit the time on a consistent basis, and without models and feedback our efforts can lack direction. Coaching cycles are a way that we can provide the partnership and structure to teachers as they work to continually improve their craft and increase student achievement.

What Is a Coaching Cycle?

Effective professional development requires continuous high-level support that can best be delivered by a school-based coach. Thomas Guskey (1995) writes, "Fitting new practices and techniques to unique on-the-job conditions is an uneven process that requires extra time and extra effort, especially when beginning. Guidance, direction, and support with pressure are crucial when these adaptations are being made" (p. 123).

It's About Time

By now many of us are familiar with Malcolm Gladwell's (2008) supposition from the book *Outliers* about how much time it takes to become good at something. He writes, "The idea that excellence at performing a complex task requires a critical minimum level of practice surfaces again and again in studies of expertise. In fact, researchers have settled on what they believe is the magic number for expertise: ten thousand hours" (p. 39). While Leanna will likely never reach a level of expertise with the ukulele (nor will she put in 10,000 hours), it's clear that when she put in the time to practice, she started to see results in her performance.

The complex task of teaching doesn't allow for isolated practice like a musical instrument does, but it still takes time to learn how to do it well.

Some may argue that excellence can only come with years and years of experience. Yet there is too much at stake for our young learners to have to wait on their teachers to gain enough experience to become effective. So we create opportunities for teachers to engage in professional learning, which serves as the "practice" that occurs in mastering other types of tasks. However, despite major financial resources invested in such learning opportunities, often very little of it leads to a change in instructional practice, let alone increased learning for students. We know from the research of Linda Darling-Hammond and her colleagues (2017) that professional learning needs to be focused and sustained over a period of weeks, months, or even an entire academic year for it to have an impact on teaching practices and student learning. Like Leanna and the ukulele, we are unlikely to get better at something when our efforts lack focus and consistency.

If the outcome of coaching is improved student learning, then coaching has to be in-depth and sustained over time. It requires a coach and teacher (or team of teachers) to determine where the students are in their learning, design and implement instruction that is differentiated, and modify the instruction to ensure that the students meet the standards. One way to provide the necessary support is by organizing coaching into cycles to create a structure that allows for sustained collaboration over a period of time. These coaching cycles provide a framework for designing ongoing and in-depth work with teachers. They occur in the six stages outlined in Figure 2.1.

When our coaching work is episodic and feels like we are always helping "one person, one time, with one thing," we call this *drive-by coaching*. It is more relationship and resource driven, and it's difficult to have a significant impact on student or teacher learning. When we provide time and focus through coaching cycles, it enables real learning to occur.

Coaching cycles have the following characteristics:

- They involve in-depth work with a small group, a pair, or an individual teacher.
- They focus on a goal for student learning that is driven by the standards.
- They last approximately four to six weeks and are typically tied to a unit of study.

- They include at least one weekly thirty- to forty-five-minute planning session to analyze student work and design instruction.

- They include one to three times per week for the coach to be in the classroom to co-teach (notice and name, think aloud, teach in tandem, you pick four, or micro-model).

FIGURE 2.1   Stages in a Coaching Cycle

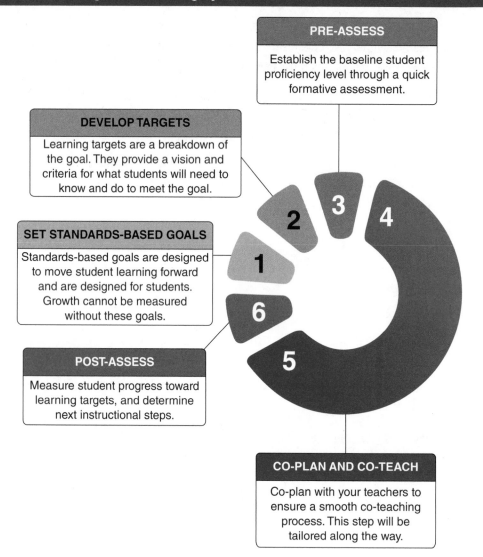

PRE-ASSESS

Establish the baseline student proficiency level through a quick formative assessment.

DEVELOP TARGETS

Learning targets are a breakdown of the goal. They provide a vision and criteria for what students will need to know and do to meet the goal.

SET STANDARDS-BASED GOALS

Standards-based goals are designed to move student learning forward and are designed for students. Growth cannot be measured without these goals.

POST-ASSESS

Measure student progress toward learning targets, and determine next instructional steps.

CO-PLAN AND CO-TEACH

Co-plan with your teachers to ensure a smooth co-teaching process. This step will be tailored along the way.

Scheduling Coaching Cycles

Though it will vary widely from coach to coach and from school to school, when the majority of coach's time is spent in cycles, their schedule will look something like Figure 2.2. It may feel challenging to pull all of the various components of a coaching cycle into a manageable schedule, but this example from a middle school coach demonstrates how it can be done. We'll also address ways to make time for coaching cycles later in this chapter.

Adapt Cycles to Meet Specific Needs

While we have witnessed many coaches having incredible success organizing their coaching this way, we also know that not everyone's role or situation is perfectly suited to following each of the components above. So we invite you to treat this as a guide rather than a set of hard-and-fast rules. For example, if curricular units at your school last three weeks, then shorten your cycles. If you're using a new math resource, it may make sense to co-plan every day since the teacher and coach are getting to know the new program. If your position is district-wide and you work across schools in early childhood, technology, or English language learning (ELL), you may choose to do more of your planning virtually through a shared online document.

Another strategy we recommend is the use of mini cycles. This structure still has the key elements of a coaching cycle. It begins with a goal or learning target and includes the collection of student evidence, co-planning, co-teaching, and reflection. The difference is that instead of going through the co-planning and co-teaching cycle over several weeks, those pieces happen closer in succession. Thus, the duration of the cycle is shortened to two to three weeks instead of four to six weeks. Figure 2.3 introduces the stages of a mini coaching cycle.

Mini cycles are useful in a variety of settings. Perhaps you are a behavior coach who works across schools, or you work at a large high school and have only a few hours a day for coaching; mini cycles may be a good fit. Another use for mini cycles is to expose teachers to this way of coaching so that they better understand the philosophy and the model. Then the goal is to shift to longer cycles as soon as teachers are ready.

FIGURE 2.2   Middle School Coaching Schedule

Key Elements to Notice:

- The coach teaches advisory and one class.
- There are three cycles happening at once (one group, two individual).
- Every cycle includes one to three times each week for co-teaching.
- When the coach works with a group (ELA team), she rotates her time in classrooms.
- Every cycle includes at least one co-planning session each week.
- The coach has time for informal coaching.
- The coach plans with the principal each week.
- The coach attends a district coach meeting each week.

	MONDAY	TUESDAY	WEDNESDAY	THURSDAY	FRIDAY
7:30–8:00	Advisory with Eighth Graders				
8:00–9:00	Teach Pre-Algebra				
9:10–10:10	Coaching Meeting	Cycle #1 with Joe: Co-teaching (math)	Cycle #1 with Joe: Co-teaching (math)	Cycle #1 with Joe: Co-teaching (math)	Cycle #2 with Chelsea: Weekly co-planning
10:20–11:30		Cycle #3 with ELA Team: Weekly co-planning	Cycle #2 with Chelsea: Co-teaching (SS)	Cycle #3 with ELA Team: Weekly co-planning	Cycle #2 with Chelsea: Co-teaching (SS)
11:30–12:00	Lunch				
12:10–1:00	Informal Coaching				
1:10–2:00	Cycle #1 with Joe: Weekly co-planning	Cycle #3 with ELA team: Co-teaching with Sarah	Weekly meeting with the principal	Cycle #3 with ELA team: Co-teaching with Mike	Cycle #3 with ELA team: Co-teaching with Dave
2:10–3:00	Prep for Coaching and Pre-Algebra				

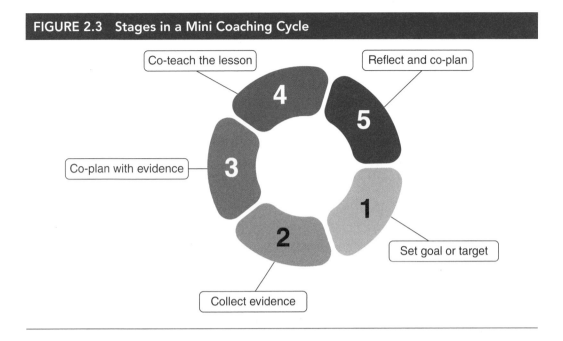

FIGURE 2.3   Stages in a Mini Coaching Cycle

While mini cycles may be useful, we recommend for coaches to work in full coaching cycles as much as possible. This is because traditional coaching cycles are designed to measure how teaching and learning is impacted, which takes time. Secondly, when coaching cycles span a unit of study, they go deeper and are more academic in nature.

No matter what modifications you choose to make, your coaching will be more impactful if you utilize the structure of cycles. Ultimately, coaching cycles help us be intentional by focusing on a single outcome for student learning and by devoting the time it takes to partner with teachers to help all students reach that goal.

Making Time for Coaching Cycles

Successfully making the switch from drive-by coaching to coaching in cycles starts with a commitment from the school leadership. If there is not an expectation that coaching cycles are happening, nor is there a master schedule to support that expectation, then it will be difficult for a coach to get into meaningful cycles with teachers.

The first step is to take a look at the master schedule. Is it structured in a way that allows for teacher collaboration? We all know that there are limited resources for teachers with regard to planning time, and it can feel like this is completely out of our control. The problem is made even worse when teachers' prep periods are not aligned with their teammates, so those who want to engage in coaching in groups don't even have the option to do so. While it's true that there are only so many hours in a day, we have seen many examples of administrators and school leadership teams thinking out of the box and getting creative with scheduling in order to free up more time for collaboration. They do so by considering questions such as the following:

- Are teachers taking on responsibilities such as lunch and recess duty? Is there a way to rotate some of these so that teachers have fewer obligations during the time they are working in coaching cycles?

- How can we make shifts in the master schedule in order for teachers to have common planning time with their teammates?

- How are we offering choice and personalization in our early release and other professional learning time? Can we think flexibly about this time so that some of it can be used for coaching cycles?

- How can we leverage "creative coverage" to create more planning time for teachers engaging in coaching cycles? (It sends a very powerful message when a principal covers for a teacher working with a coach.)

In addition to creating a master schedule that supports coaching cycles, coaches and their administrators also need to be mindful of everything that ends up on a coach's plate. When a coaching program is new and the role is undefined, a coach may get tasked with everything from being the testing coordinator, emergency substitute, small-group interventionist, resource room manager, and data analyst—leaving them with little to no time for actual coaching. The best way to combat this is suggested by Sweeney and Mausbach (2018) in *Leading Student-Centered Coaching: Building Principal and Coach Partnerships*:

> One of our favorite systems for protecting the coach's role is regular calendar reviews with the principal. The ideal time for this to occur is every four to six weeks. This helps coaches

craft a new calendar as they launch a new round of coaching cycles. Checking in at the beginning of the new round provides the principal with the opportunity to make sure that the coach is mostly in coaching cycles. It's also a way to help the coach achieve balance between duties that are coaching related and duties that might be for another purpose. (p. 50)

Committing to Coaching Cycles

When a coach's schedule is regularly analyzed in this way, it keeps the focus on prioritizing his or her time to have the biggest impact possible on student achievement. That said, we still find that even when administrators assist in protecting the coach's time, there can be another factor getting in the way and that is the coach themselves.

Maria was in her third year of coaching at a rural elementary school in Wyoming. She was well regarded by her colleagues and valued at the school by both teachers and her principal. In fact, you could say she was indispensable—seemingly ubiquitous in every conversation, committee, and initiative throughout the school.

While she managed to eke out time to engage in a few coaching cycles here and there, Maria found these to be highly productive and impactful on both teacher and student learning. She often complained that she wished she had more time for coaching cycles, but when pushed to examine her schedule by her colleagues in their coaching PLC, she was steadfast in her rationalization: "There is nothing that can be taken off my plate. We're a small school with limited resources. If I don't do these things, then no one will." There was certainly some truth to that; she was always the first one everyone went to when they were in a bind and something needed to get done. While she would have liked more time to coach, it also felt good to be so valued and needed by everyone.

It felt like a punch in the gut when Maria got some not-so-positive feedback from a teacher at the end of a coaching cycle. "I don't think our time together was as productive as it could have been because of how often we had to cancel our co-planning and co-teaching sessions. I didn't feel very valued in the process." This stung. She didn't want to always be canceling, but she also felt she couldn't say no when asked to help in other areas that seemed to need urgent attention. One of her fellow coaches offered an idea: "If you have time scheduled with a teacher and you get asked to do something else, explain that you have a current commitment and ask if you can help with the other issue later. You don't have to say no, but you can say not now." The next time emergency class coverage was needed, Maria tried this strategy and, a bit to her surprise, it worked. Someone else was found to cover the class, and she could keep her commitment to the teacher she was coaching. It didn't take long before these types of requests for her time became fewer and fewer. It felt bittersweet to give up her role as a key helper at the school, but once she demonstrated that coaching was her number one priority, everyone else in the building began to follow suit. She still stayed involved with lots of committees and initiatives, but she was able to let go of some things and free up a lot more time for herself to engage in the impactful coaching cycle work.

This experience was a valuable learning opportunity for Maria. When we make time for coaching cycles to happen, both schoolwide and for the individual coach, it allows for deep and meaningful work to take place.

What About Curriculum, Programs, and Classroom Management?

We know that coaching cycles take time and that we have to intentionally make time for them to happen. Coaching cycles may feel like they compete with other things happening in the school, such as implementing new curriculum, other school or district initiatives, or classroom management and behavior issues. So we need to find a way to make everything work together. There is no doubt that teachers and schools are being pulled in many different directions. As was discussed in Chapter 1, coaching should never be viewed as "one more thing." So the challenge becomes how to make all of these other things fit within the coaching cycle structure, like meeting the requirements of a prescribed curriculum or initiative, for example, while still focusing over time on a goal for student learning.

The first step is making sure we separate the *goal* for learning from the *resources* we use in order to meet the goal. In other words, using a certain program in reading, implementing a workshop structure in math, using a Quizlet for real-time formative assessment in biology, or utilizing Socratic Seminar for discussions in a US history class should never be viewed as goals in and of themselves. The goal should always be about student learning. We start by asking, "What do students need to know and be able to do" in reading, math, science, or history. Once we've determined the goal, then we can think about what tools will help us get there—be it a reading program, a classroom structure, a tech platform, or a discussion protocol.

Addressing Behavior and Classroom Management Within Coaching Cycles

In addition to considering curriculum and programs in coaching cycles, we often find that classroom management and behavior are major concerns. Certainly there are times when it feels like the proverbial house is on fire and that until the management issue gets under control no real learning can happen. In these cases it makes sense to give some targeted, more teacher-centered support over a short period of time. Oftentimes, however, these issues can be addressed holistically in the coaching cycle.

This was the case with Randi and Ian, who were working on the goal *Students will compare multiple texts to analyze how similar themes and topics are addressed* with Ian's sophomore American Literature class. Ian had shared frustrations about student behavior in the past, so Randi wanted to make sure this was addressed up front in their planning. She asked Ian, "What behaviors will need to be in place for the students to be successful?" Ian said that they would need to be better at staying on task when working independently. Randi replied with "What if we built in some strategies for this as well?" Ian seemed relieved that he and Randi could focus on both academics and behavior at the same time.

Structuring coaching in this way reminds us that having students behave in class isn't the end goal but rather a necessary component for kids to be successful in their learning. We can support teachers in improving their classroom management practices as a means to the particular learning goal we are working on together in a coaching cycle.

In practice, keeping the focus on student learning takes perseverance on the part of the coach. When a teacher comes to us asking for help with things like practices, structures, and management, it's tempting to want to drop everything to jump in and help. But if we believe in the value of coaching with a single learning focus over an extended period of time, then we need to have language to both validate the teacher's request while at the same time making the case for more intentional work in coaching cycles. Figure 2.6 at the end of the chapter gives us language to help teachers see how working in coaching cycles shouldn't be a separate effort from all the other things they want—and need—to be working on.

What About Coaching Cycles With Groups?

In the sample schedule in Figure 2.2, we see that one of the coaching cycles is with a group of three English language arts (ELA) teachers. To make coaching with a group or team logistically feasible and cohesive for all of the participants, the coach blocks out one time per week to co-teach with each of the participants in the group, and then the entire group has at least one common planning time. While these scheduling guidelines seem simple enough, there are some other important nuances to take into consideration when thinking about how coaching cycles work with groups.

A question we often get asked by coaches is what to do when there is a challenging dynamic among a team or not all members of a team choose to participate in a coaching cycle. In these cases our answer is "Don't force it." We use the language of coaching *groups* because it implies that a group may or may not include every member of a team. Sometimes the group consists of part of the team, and occasionally it is made up of members of different grade levels or subject areas. As long as everyone is working on a common goal for students and is committed to the process, coaching groups can be an incredibly productive structure. For example, this structure may prove useful when working in small schools with only one teacher per grade level or in schools that are committed to vertical teaming. As for those reluctant team members? They often end up joining once they see all the great learning that's taking place.

Is a Group Cycle the Same as a PLC?

Coaches and administrators also wonder what the difference is between coaching cycles with groups and PLCs. If a coach is involved with PLCs, isn't it basically the same as group coaching? The two structures certainly do have a lot in common. Yet while it would be convenient to think that they are one and the same, Figure 2.4 demonstrates that there are some very distinct differences between them.

FIGURE 2.4　Group Coaching Cycles Compared to PLCs

WHAT GROUP COACHING CYCLES AND PLCs HAVE IN COMMON

- Guided by roughly the same four questions
  - Where are students now?
  - What do they need to know?
  - How will we know if they get there?
  - What will we do for those who don't?
- Take place with a small group of teachers
- Student evidence is always present
- Guided by standards
- Use ongoing formative assessments

QUALITIES THAT ARE UNIQUE TO GROUP COACHING CYCLES	QUALITIES UNIQUE TO PLCs
• Teachers choose a subject area and content focus of the goal • Teachers choose who participates in the group • Shorter in duration • Co-teaching is integral to the process • Guided by a coach	• Often mandated by school administration • Ongoing • Group doesn't change • No in-classroom component • May or may not involve a coach

As Figure 2.4 illustrates, there are some clear differences between group coaching cycles and PLCs. Rather than one being a replacement for the other, they have tremendous potential to both inform and enhance each other. Viewing cycles and PLCs in this way helps align professional learning and keep the focus on "the thing," as discussed in Chapter 1. Coaches should think flexibly and intentionally about how they move between PLCs and group cycles to help everyone get the most out of these powerful professional learning structures.

Lesson From the Field

Monica was among the first group of instructional coaches hired when her district received a grant to support mathematics instruction. Early on, she knew that building relationships would be important, so she started there. She made a point of frequently popping into teachers' rooms to see how they were doing and if they needed help with anything. She took requests for all kinds of things from brainstorming ideas to increase math fluency with a third-grade team to helping a kindergarten teacher cut out shapes for an upcoming math activity. Monica also spent time helping teachers understand the math curriculum through lesson planning and professional development. While she wasn't always sure where to put her efforts, she felt that she was making some headway. Teachers seemed to value working with her, and even though her work lacked focus, she was definitely keeping busy.

Halfway through her first year, Monica attended a professional development meeting for coaches at the district office. The team was asked to go through their calendars and report how they were spending their time. This information would then be used to evaluate the implementation of the grant program. When Tonia, the district leader in charge of the initiative, broached the subject of providing this information the anxiety became palpable. There were eight coaches on the team, and most of them weren't sure how to respond. Expectations about how they should spend their time hadn't been clearly defined, and yet suddenly it seemed they were being judged by this metric. Once the coaches turned in their data it became clear that, like Monica, the team was spending most of their time in the following areas:

- Providing resources to teachers

- Meeting with teachers to plan isolated lessons

- Providing professional development focused on the math curriculum

- Performing "other duties"—pulling small groups, managing testing, etc.

The grant providers wanted to know how the coaches' activities were impacting student achievement. In reviewing the current duties most coaches were engaged in, they honestly weren't sure how to answer this question. Like Monica, all of the coaches were busy *helping* teachers, but they weren't able to pinpoint how coaching was specifically impacting learning.

Tonia realized the grant demanded a different kind of coaching. Through her study of Student-Centered Coaching, she learned that they could focus more directly on outcomes for student learning. They shifted their model to include coaching cycles, and the group was encouraged to begin with one teacher and then increase over time.

Not quite knowing where to start, Monica approached Jeff, a veteran fifth-grade teacher with whom she had a particularly strong relationship. She explained the idea of a coaching cycle—that they would set a goal for student learning and then work together through co-planning and co-teaching over the next five weeks to help kids meet it. Monica and Jeff identified two times a week when they would co-plan, and Jeff picked two days of the week he thought it would be best to have Monica in the classroom with him. Monica admitted that this was all new to her and that they would be learning together every step of the way.

When they set a goal for the cycle, they both realized that focusing on the standards felt different from what they had done in the past. Rather than discussing specific instructional practices, they started with how Jeff's fifth graders were performing as mathematicians and where he hoped they would be by the end of the upcoming unit. This provided a sense of energy and optimism that they hadn't felt before. Monica asked questions like "What do you think it will take for your students to meet the goal?" and "What will success look like?" These kinds of questions kept their conversations anchored in student learning.

Monica began to see a difference as she engaged in regular co-planning and co-teaching with Jeff. At first she wasn't clear what her role was in his classroom, but with time they became more comfortable working together to meet students' needs. They often conferred with one another during the lesson; in this way they could compare notes about what they were seeing and what they thought should happen next. Monica knew she still had a lot to learn about coaching, but this sure did feel more meaningful that what she had been doing before.

When the coaching cycle wrapped up, they gave the class the end-of-unit assessment. What they found was that Jeff's students grew tremendously compared to where they were five weeks before. It was clear that a few students would still need some support, and Monica helped Jeff think through what this would look like, even as the class was ready to move on to the next unit. Overall, they were both thrilled with how many kids mastered the standards that were taught.

With this experience, Monica began to view her work differently. Spending time with one teacher over a period of time, with a focus on a goal for student learning, made it clear that she could have an impact. Jeff also expressed that the coaching cycle was a great learning experience, and he began regularly incorporating things he had done with Monica into his everyday planning and teaching. Monica was still spending some of her time providing professional development and resources to teachers, but she loved how much more impactful her coaching felt working in a cycle. Little by little word got out to other teachers about the positive work she had done with Jeff, and this led to more coaching cycles in the coming months.

Later in the year, the team met with Tonia, and the topic of impacting student achievement came up again. Monica and the rest of the coaches noticed that what had previously been a stressful meeting felt a lot more like a celebration, as everyone on the team had completed at least one coaching cycle by that point in time. They all realized that organizing their coaching in this way allowed them to provide a high level of support to teachers while making sure that the work stayed focused on student learning. It felt great!

Tools and Techniques

Coaching cycles provide a system through which coaches and teachers can engage in meaningful work toward increasing student achievement. They start with identifying a goal for student learning and culminate with measuring both student and teacher learning. In thinking of each phase of a cycle, it is helpful to have some questions to guide us. We recommend using these questions and logs authentically. This creates responsive conversations that are efficient and go deep—all at the same time. Figure 2.5 is a series of coaching logs that can help with that process.

As we discussed earlier in this chapter, teachers may feel inundated with issues they're facing in the classroom, such as implementing new programs or dealing with behavior issues. Naturally, these needs will come to the forefront in coaching conversations, so we want to be equipped with language to help us validate their wishes while helping them see the benefit of working in coaching cycles (see Figure 2.6). The if/then charts at the end of each chapter can also be found in Resource A in this book.

FIGURE 2.5   Student-Centered Coaching Logs

COACHING LOG: SET STANDARDS-BASED GOALS

Guiding Questions:

1. What is the goal for student learning for this coaching cycle? What do we hope the students will learn as a result of our partnership?

2. Is there any data that will inform us as we set a goal?

3. What standard(s) does this goal address?

4. Is there a specific unit in the curriculum that the goal addresses?

Notes and Next Steps:

COACHING LOG: UNPACK THE GOAL INTO LEARNING TARGETS

Guiding Questions:

1. What are the learning targets (or success criteria) that will help the students reach the goal?

2. Do the learning targets address a balance of *know, understand,* and *do*? Do they go beyond lessons and activities?

3. Are there any behavior targets that we want to include?

4. Are the targets written in student-friendly language?

Notes and Next Steps:

COACHING LOG: CREATE A PLAN FOR THE PRE-ASSESSMENT

Guiding Questions:

1. How will we assess the students to measure growth across the coaching cycle? We can use an existing assessment or create our own.

2. Is the assessment open-ended and descriptive in nature?

3. Does the assessment align with the learning targets?

4. When will we meet again to analyze the data that we collect?

Notes and Next Steps:

(Continued)

FIGURE 2.5 (Continued)

COACHING LOG: DOCUMENT BASELINE DATA

Guiding Questions:

1. How did the students perform on the pre-assessment?

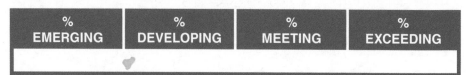

% EMERGING	% DEVELOPING	% MEETING	% EXCEEDING

2. Does the data indicate any ways in which we should modify or prioritize the learning targets? If so, how?

3. Based on the data, what is our first step in instruction?

Notes and Next Steps:

COACHING LOG: CO-PLAN WITH STUDENT EVIDENCE

Guiding Questions:

1. What is the learning target for the lesson?

2. How will students demonstrate their understanding of the target?

3. How would we want students to answer the following questions:
   - What am I learning?
   - Why am I learning it?
   - How will I know when I have learned it?

4. Do we have evidence from the last lesson that will inform how we can differentiate instruction?

5. What resources and materials will we need to prepare?

6. How will we work together to manage student behavior?

Planner for Sharing Lessons

WHAT'S HAPPENING?	WHAT WILL IT LOOK LIKE?	WHO WILL TAKE THE LEAD? WHAT WILL THE OTHER "TEACHER" DO?

Notes and Next Steps:

COACHING LOG: EVIDENCE OF TEACHER AND STUDENT LEARNING

Guiding Questions:

1. How did students perform on the post-assessment?

% EMERGING	% DEVELOPING	% MEETING	% EXCEEDING

2. What support will be given to students who did not meet the goal?

3. How have you grown professionally as a result of the coaching?

4. How can I continue to support you even though the cycle is finished?

Notes and Next Steps:

online resources   Available for download at **resources.corwin.com/EssentialGuideforSCCoaching**

FIGURE 2.6   Language for Connecting Coaching Cycles With Curriculum, Programs, and Classroom Management

IF I HEAR . . .	THEN I CAN USE THE FOLLOWING LANGUAGE . . .
"I don't have time for a whole coaching cycle. I just want you to show me how to use more technology in my classroom since our principal has been pushing for that."	"I'm happy to help you figure out how to use more technology. Tell me a bit more about what unit you have coming up. It would be great to partner on planning and teaching the actual unit, and we can think about what different tech tools will support student learning along the way."
"I'm not sure why we need to decide on a goal for students when the curriculum scope and sequence have everything mapped out for us. If you can just come in and model a couple of lessons for me, that would be great."	"The new reading curriculum definitely has a tight pacing guide. I think that if we look through the upcoming unit, we'll be able to pull out the big ideas that are tied to the standards. We can use that to help kids engage in the end goal, and we can work together to monitor their progress and make adjustments along the way. This will help us be more intentional as we learn the new curriculum together."

(Continued)

FIGURE 2.6   (Continued)

IF I HEAR . . .	THEN I CAN USE THE FOLLOWING LANGUAGE . . .
"Since we're working on a new behavior initiative, it seems like that should be the focus of what we work on together."	"There is definitely an expectation that we are all working on the new behavior program with students. But we still need to be helping them meet the standards as well. How about if we think of a goal for student learning and then figure out what behaviors from the program the kids will need to be successful in the learning? Then you and I can partner over the next several weeks to embed those things into our teaching to help your students meet the goal."

A Final Thought

Teaching is hard work, and there is no step-by-step manual to follow that explains how to be a master teacher. In order to improve our craft we must put in the time and intention—always with a focus on outcomes for students. Student-Centered Coaching cycles provide a platform to engage in this kind of professional learning. The coach is a partner in supporting teacher and student learning, and the structure ensures in-depth collaboration.

When getting started with Student-Centered Coaching, it can be challenging for a coach to get into cycles. We understand that it can take time to get the message out and to make cultural shifts for this kind of coaching to take root. Coaching cycles are the bedrock of Student-Centered Coaching, upon which meaningful and measurable learning is able to take place. In the following chapters we will discuss a variety of things to take into account in order to make them happen.

Understanding
Our Impact

3

//

Several years ago, Leanna was hired for the newly created position of instructional coach in a K–12 charter school in Denver. It was an innovative and exciting place to be and was staffed by a group of talented and dedicated professionals. Everyone from the principal to the secretary were committed to the school's mission, and for Leanna it felt like the perfect place to work. As was common back then, Leanna's role wasn't well defined, so she took it upon herself to figure out what to do when school started. As a way of getting to know all of the teachers, she visited each of their classrooms to observe them and give some feedback. Then when the kindergarten teacher had to administer individual reading assessments, Leanna offered to cover his class over several days so it could get done. She set up a welcoming professional resource room for the staff and worked with the principal to plan their weekly after school staff meetings. It felt like she was off to a good start.

Once everyone got settled after the first few weeks of school, there were a few teachers who expressed interest in working with their new coach. To create choice and ownership (and not really knowing what else to do), Leanna let them know she was available to help with whatever they needed. Occasionally this involved planning units or individual lessons. Often teachers wanted resources and ideas—about everything from a good book to use as a mentor text for an upcoming writing unit to strategies for classroom management. Sometimes they just stopped in her office to chat about the challenges of being a teacher. Rarely, if ever, did any of this involve looking at student work.

As the year went on, Leanna continued to work mostly with that initial group. Occasionally she would try to engage with a few of the more reluctant teachers, but typically this was met with comments like "Thanks, but now is not a good time." While this was frustrating, she didn't have the slightest clue of what she could do to change the situation.

When she reflected on whether or not she was making a difference, Leanna wasn't quite sure what to think. How should she define her success? On the one hand there was the group of teachers who were eager to work with her and with whom she had created strong and trusting relationships. But then there was the rest of the staff who didn't want to engage with her either personally or professionally. She felt like she was making some progress, but how could she really know?

Fast forward about ten years, and Leanna found herself in an online Twitter chat for instructional coaches. The moderator posted the question, "How do you know you are having success as a coach?" Leanna was curious to see the responses since she had asked herself the same question over the years. Some responses were heartfelt and others a bit more self-deprecating, and included:

I know I'm successful as a coach when . . .

- people sit with me in the staff lounge.
- teachers ask me for help with things.
- I get "repeat customers."
- people don't run the other way when they see me coming down the hall!

These comments reflected the same thoughts Leanna had all those years ago. They were largely based on the notion of coaching being about relationships (I'm successful if they *like* me) and being a resource (I'm successful if they want *help* from me) and not at all about making an impact on students.

Why We Need to Know Our Impact

It is not uncommon to hear coaches thinking about success in terms of the ideas expressed previously. Through our work with Student-Centered Coaching, our own thoughts have grown to include the following principles:

- Our coaching work must impact student learning.

- Relationships are a critical component but not the end goal of our work.

- We need a tangible system for measuring our impact.

In Chapter 1 we discussed the Visible Learning research and John Hattie's exhortation to "know thy impact." He writes, "Teachers and school leaders need to be critical evaluators of the effect that they are having on their students" (Hattie, 2012, p. 5). It is not enough to know that something is having an impact; rather, we need to know what is having the biggest and most profound impact possible on our students' learning.

A second reason for knowing our impact is accountability. As school districts invest in instructional coaches, they must be able to demonstrate "that these efforts are valuable to the school organization, to individual educators, and, ultimately, to students" (Guskey, 2000, p. 8). School board members, district administrators, legislators, and members of the school community should all be able to know whether or not the investment in coaching is making a difference.

Lastly, coaches need to know their impact for their own sense of self-efficacy. It's hard to imagine that anyone who puts time and energy into something does so without caring about their performance. Coaches, like all educators, are a passionate and dedicated bunch. When they are unable to receive validation that what they're doing is having an impact, it can lead to disillusion and dissatisfaction with the job. Sadly, we've seen several coaches leave the position over the years for this very reason.

Measure Growth by Pre- and Post-Assessing

The primary way we can measure our impact is by collecting pre- and post-assessment data during coaching cycles. This enables us to have a clear picture of how students have grown in their learning and understanding of the goal for the cycle. In *Student-Centered Coaching: The Moves*, we note that "the assessments we use have several qualities in order to be manageable and meaningful for teachers and coaches. They are efficient, provide descriptive insight into student thinking and understanding, and are aligned with the learning targets and goal for students"

(Sweeney & Harris, 2017, p. 136). This means they are formative in nature rather than a list of problems to solve or fill-in-the-blank questions to answer. We look holistically at the evidence collected to get a sense of where students are starting in relation to the goal. Designing assessments with these qualities helps teachers see the power of using pre- and post-assessments as an instructional tool that enables us to measure growth over the course of the coaching cycle.

Yet sometimes teachers still see pre-assessing as a waste of time. Therefore, it can be helpful to point out that pre-assessments have several benefits in addition to providing baseline data. As Guskey and McTighe (2016) explain, these include identifying the prior knowledge students bring to the learning, focusing attention on the learning targets, and uncovering any misconceptions they may have. The idea is not to assess discreet content that the students likely don't yet know. When we structure the pre-assessment to be descriptive and have multiple entry points, we gain valuable information about what schema the students already have as well as any misconceptions that may exist. It also gives us baseline data to measure student growth from beginning to end. Making these assessments user-friendly and highlighting the ways in which we can use the data helps teachers to see that pre-assessing is indeed a valuable use of instructional time.

On the back end, we post-assess students when the cycle is finished in order to measure growth. These assessments match our pre-assessments as closely as possible so we can get the most accurate measurement of student growth. This can be the percentage of students who met the goal or a more nuanced view of how many were emerging, developing, meeting, or exceeding the goal at the beginning of the coaching cycle compared to at the end. This practice leads to many opportunities to celebrate student growth and plan for those who still need our support.

Use Continuous Formative Assessment to Understand Our Impact

Many of us have had the experience of receiving an unfortunate surprise when we gave the end-of-unit test. We plodded along through the unit, thinking our students were "getting it," only to have most of them perform poorly at the end. How could this have happened? Almarode and

Vandas (2018) point out in *Clarity for Learning: Five Essential Practices That Empower Students and Teachers*:

> As learners engage in the learning process, the successful progression of learning involves monitoring formative assessment and effective feedback. However, if we do not offer students opportunities to recall, reorganize, and make meaning of their learning, or we do not give them opportunities to make their thinking visible, we cannot adjust instruction to support their learning, and they are not able to think about their learning and make their own adjustments as self-directed learners. (p. 22)

On the other hand, with a clear goal and success criteria, coaches and teachers are able to formatively assess students throughout coaching cycles. When we co-plan with teachers each week, we use evidence to see where students are relative to the goal. We then use that information to plan instruction that is responsive to the students' needs. When we co-teach, we embed formative assessment into moves like *Noticing and Naming* and *You Pick Four* (Sweeney & Harris, 2017) to obtain an in-the-moment understanding of where students are in their learning. In this way we are able to see how students are progressing and then make necessary adjustments in instruction along the way. By monitoring the impact of our work every step of the way, we aren't met with surprises at the end because we already have a clear picture of where students are as learners and the steps we've taken to help get them there.

Measuring Impact With the Results-Based Coaching Tool

Even with formative assessment practices built into the model for Student-Centered Coaching, it hasn't always been easy to demonstrate the connection between coaching and student achievement. Diane faced this dilemma when she was working with a school district in Missouri a number of years ago.

The school board wanted proof that coaching was making a difference with students—a fair request given the fact that the district had invested a significant amount of resources to hire eighteen instructional coaches across their elementary, middle, and high schools. In thinking about how to develop a system to measure their impact, she knew that whatever she came up with had to reinforce their coaching practice and fit seamlessly into their daily work with teachers and students. She also wanted to be sure that something empirical came from the data so that the coaches could present the school board with the "hard data" they were requesting. So she took the basic structure of the coaching cycle and bookended it with pre- and post-assessments to create the Results-Based Coaching Tool (RBCT). This would make the evaluation process more concrete and offer the coaches a seamless way to measure the impact of their coaching.

When Diane presented the tool to the team, they raised the roof with choruses of "This is what I've needed all along! Why didn't you bring this to us sooner?" They felt it reinforced the types of conversations they were having with teachers and provided a natural flow and rhythm that they could repeat again and again. Rather than becoming a distraction from their work, they recognized how it would help them stay focused on the steps of the coaching cycle while giving them concrete evidence of how their work was affecting students.

Since Diane created that first version all those years ago, the RBCT has been continually modified and enhanced by coaches in the field. In order to best understand the tool and how it is used, we have broken it down and explained each section in Figure 3.1. A full version of the RBCT can be found in Resource B in at the end of this book.

Collect Anecdotal Evidence Through Exit Interviews

In *Student-Centered Coaching: The Moves* (Sweeney & Harris, 2017), we wrote about the importance of creating opportunities for reflection to collect evidence of teacher growth from coaching. While there are many chances to do this informally throughout the coaching cycle, we find that the most powerful way is through an exit interview at the end of the cycle. "Though some coaches feel that conducting such an interview seems awkwardly formal, we believe that intentionally doing so creates both a space for reflection and an opportunity to capture evidence that comes directly from teachers themselves instead of from us as their coaches" (Sweeney, 2011, p. 139).

FIGURE 3.1　The Results-Based Coaching Tool Deconstructed and Annotated

Standards-Based Goal What is the goal for student learning?	
Students will . . .	← Using the language "students will" helps us stay focused on the fact that our goal is about learning rather than a teaching strategy or structure.
Standard(s):	← Sometimes a goal will align specifically with one particular standard; often several standards or parts of standards are addressed at once.
Learning Targets: I can:	← The goal is broken down into a set of learning targets, or success criteria, which will guide instruction throughout the coaching cycle and which will be used to formatively assess along the way.
Baseline Data: ___ Emerging ___ Developing ___ Meeting ___ Exceeding ___ % of students were able to demonstrate proficiency of the learning targets	← A pre-assessment is given in order to determine baseline data and to see what understanding students are already bringing to the learning. The descriptors can be modified to match specific school or district language.

Focus for Teacher Learning What instructional practices will help students reach the goal?	
Teacher will . . .	← This section is where thinking is held about all of the strategies, structures, resources, and activities that might be used throughout the coaching cycle in order to help students reach the goal. This can include things the teacher says they want to work on (e.g., setting up a readers' workshop) as well as school or district expectations (such as implementing the new math curriculum). The list can be added to as new thinking is generated throughout the coaching cycle.

(Continued)

FIGURE 3.1   (Continued)

Student-Centered Coaching	
What coaching practices were implemented during this coaching cycle?	
Coach and Teacher did . . . (check all that apply) ☐ Goal setting ☐ Creating learning targets ☐ Analysis of student work ☐ Co-teaching ☐ Collecting student evidence during the class period ☐ Collaborative planning ☐ Shared learning to build knowledge of content and pedagogy ☐ Other _____	⬅ Here the coach can keep track of all of the different ways they collaborate with the teacher(s) during the coaching cycle. It also serves as a way to help teachers understand what to expect the coach to be doing (and not be doing) in a cycle.

Teacher Learning	
As a result of the coaching cycle, what instructional practices are being used on a consistent basis?	
Teacher is . . .	⬅ This is where the teacher can reflect on his or her own learning and growth as a result of the coaching cycle. It can be generated from time in the classroom or from reflection at the end of the coaching cycle. It is important to note that this is not a place for evaluation but rather for celebration. Most of the thinking should come from the teacher.

Student Learning	
How did student learning increase as a result of the coaching cycle?	
Students are . . .	⬅ Anecdotal evidence can be shared about how students have grown in their learning and can be recorded here. It may be specific to the learning targets or it may be more general, such as reflections about an increased level of student engagement for example.

Post-Assessment Data: ____ Emerging ____ Developing ____ Meeting ____ Exceeding ____ % of students were able to demonstrate proficiency of the learning targets	← The post-assessment should mirror the pre-assessment as closely as possible in order to adequately measure growth.
Follow-up for students who didn't reach the goal:	← There may be a few students who didn't yet reach the goal. It is important for the coach and teacher to make sure a plan is in place to continue to support these students with the learning.

As coaches have been using the RBCT over the years, we have learned a lot from their different iterations and modifications. One big takeaway came from a team of coaches in Nevada, who decided to add the exit interview onto the end, seen in Figure 3.2. Having these reflective questions built in as part of the tool helps to set the expectation that the exit interview is an important part of the coaching cycle, and it ensures that this valuable evidence is collected to help measure the impact of coaching.

FIGURE 3.2   Exit Interview Questions on the Results-Based Coaching Tool

TEACHER REFLECTIONS	COACH REFLECTIONS
How did the coaching cycle support the students' learning?	What coaching moves most supported the coaching cycle?
Were there any challenges or missed opportunities during the coaching cycle?	Were there any challenges or missed opportunities during the coaching cycle?
What are some next steps for your teaching as a result of the coaching cycle?	What are some next steps for your coaching as a result of the coaching cycle?

Other Ways to Use the Results-Based Coaching Tool

The RBCT provides a thorough and uniform way to measure the impact on teacher and student learning from the work done in a coaching cycle.

We measure growth through pre- and post-assessment data, and we document anecdotal evidence of learning in the exit interview. This allows us to measure the impact of coaching toward a specific goal for learning with a specific group of students.

Each RBCT is packed with useful information. For this reason, there are a number of additional ways to use the tool to understand our impact. This includes using it in the context of professional learning for coaches. We do this by looking at sets of the tool individually, at the school level, or district-wide. A few of these ways we can do this are described next.

Sharing Success and Building Collective Efficacy

Throughout this book, we talk a lot about the importance of celebration. For example, some principals begin staff meetings by encouraging teachers to share a success from a coaching cycle. Others include shout-outs about teacher and student growth in their newsletters. This sends the message that "we are all learners" and creates the incentive for teachers to engage authentically in coaching.

As we discussed in Chapter 1, we know that collective teacher efficacy has one of the highest influences on student achievement at 1.39, and using the RBCT as a way of celebrating success can help build it. In the book *Collective Efficacy: How Educators' Beliefs Impact Student Learning,* Jenni Donohoo (2017) writes, "If educators' realities are filtered through the belief that they can do very little to influence student achievement, then it is very likely these beliefs will be manifested in their practice" (p. 7). She goes on to uncover that when we analyze the factors that lead to success, it helps us build a sense of collective efficacy. When we purposefully and publicly celebrate the successes that have been documented with the RBCT, we emphasize the belief that together, we *do* make a positive impact on student achievement.

Identifying Areas for Future Professional Learning and Support for Coaches

When most districts plan professional support for coaches, it typically revolves around the "stuff" of teaching and learning. This usually means they attend trainings on things like Balanced Literacy, a newly adopted content curriculum, or any of the many initiatives a district may be engaged in. It's important for coaches to be up to date and well versed in this content, but they also need support on how to do the work of coaching. When trying to hone in on specific needs for a team of coaches, the RBCT can provide valuable insights.

This was the case with a district that Diane was working with in Iowa. The group of eleven coaches were actively engaging in coaching cycles and using the tool to measure their impact, but some coaches still seemed to be struggling. They reported things such as the cycle ending after only two weeks, that they had to change the focus partway through, or that they were just coaching on whatever seemed to be a burning issue at the moment. Diane figured that since they had access to everyone's RBCTs from the past few months, these could provide some clues about what was going on. As she and Lance, the district coordinator, started looking through the data, they noticed inconsistencies in the goals for coaching cycles. Some goals focused on finite skills like *Students will learn multiplication facts through 8*. Some focused on engagement rather than on the standards, such as *Students will actively engage in math workshop*. Others seemed quite large in scope such as *Students will understand the key concepts in the chemistry curriculum*.

While Lance and Diane were pleased to see that coaches were working in cycles with teachers, looking at this evidence reminded them that starting with "Students will . . . " doesn't guarantee that the goal is learning focused, standards-based, and rigorous enough to sustain a coaching cycle. To address the issue, they decided to build this work into their next meeting with coaches. This allowed them to guide the team to think about how their goals could be made stronger. The coaches appreciated that the professional learning they were being offered was meeting a demonstrated need and that they would now have the tools to make their coaching work even more impactful moving forward.

Monitoring Focus on a Unified Goal

In Chapter 1, we discussed the importance of being clear about "the thing" schools are going after in order to align professional learning in service of student learning. Coaching cycles are one of the supports, along with things like PLCs and large-group professional development that help teachers to be successful with "the thing." In other words, coaching cycles support student learning while at the same time reinforcing effective practices in the school improvement plan.

If a school is clear about "the thing." then it should permeate all aspects of teaching and learning. One of the ways this can be monitored is by examining a set of RBCTs after a round of coaching cycles or perhaps at the end of the semester. In Figure 3.1, we saw that in the second column of the tool, the teacher and coach identify practices that will help students meet the goal. In the fourth column, the teacher identifies practices they are using on a consistent basis as a result of the coaching work. Information gathered from these two sections can help schools answer important questions such as the following:

- Are teachers and coaches focusing on "the thing" to help students reach the goal for learning?

- Are teachers reporting an increase in using "the thing" after engaging in coaching cycles?

- Is there a need for continued support through large group professional development or other learning opportunities?

When using the RBCT in this way, a school can establish a clear understanding about how they are doing with maintaining focus on a single initiative and about what further supports teachers may need in this effort.

In addition to the ways the RBCT can be used that have been explained previously, Figure 3.3 identifies how the tool can be used to understand the impact of coaching and help promote student and teacher learning. The first bubble looks at the RBCT from a single coaching cycle at a time. The second bubble focuses on a set of RBCTs from a round of coaching cycles or from a full semester at a school. The final bubble refers to using a set of RBCTs over a span of time from the whole district coaching team.

Lesson From the Field

A team of K–12 coaches were gathered at the district's Teaching and Learning Center for their monthly meeting. This was typically a time when they would participate in district professional development on certain initiatives; run their own PLC as a cohort of coaches; and get updates from Shayla, the district coordinator, on all kinds of matters that

FIGURE 3.3   Using the Results-Based Coaching Tool to Assess Implementation

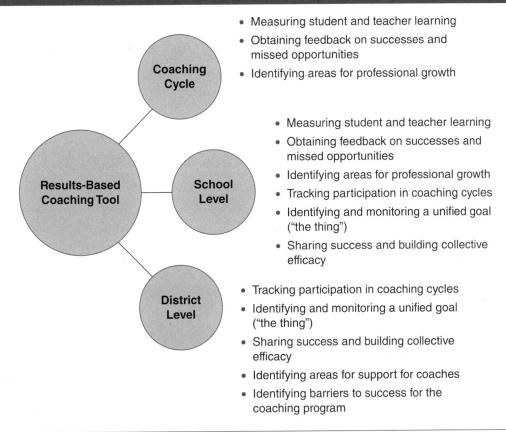

- Measuring student and teacher learning
- Obtaining feedback on successes and missed opportunities
- Identifying areas for professional growth

- Measuring student and teacher learning
- Obtaining feedback on successes and missed opportunities
- Identifying areas for professional growth
- Tracking participation in coaching cycles
- Identifying and monitoring a unified goal ("the thing")
- Sharing success and building collective efficacy

- Tracking participation in coaching cycles
- Identifying and monitoring a unified goal ("the thing")
- Sharing success and building collective efficacy
- Identifying areas for support for coaches
- Identifying barriers to success for the coaching program

related to their coaching work. On this particular day, however, there was a sense of dread hanging over the group. At the school board meeting the night before, there was discussion of impending budget cuts, and the coaching program was toward the top of this list as potentially being "on the chopping block."

The coaching team was a dedicated group of educators who had been working hard over the past three years to partner with teachers to improve student achievement. They had done book studies and attended conferences, and the district had hired Leanna to work with them to help implement Student-Centered Coaching. Each person in the group felt they were making an impact on both student and teacher learning at their respective schools, so the thought of possibly having to throw it all away felt like a giant punch in the gut.

Shayla had been at the meeting the night before, so the group looked to her for more information. "Some board members were questioning whether the investment in coaching is worth it," she shared. "They said they aren't sure that coaches are having much of an impact on student learning." This second comment elicited quite a reaction from the group. "How can they say that when we have evidence to show the difference we're making? Has anyone ever showed them our RBCTs?" one of the coaches asked. Tensions were running high, as the coaches were feeling frustrated and betrayed by the lack of confidence expressed by these school board members.

As a strong leader and trusted ally, Shayla tried to calm the coaches and move them in a productive direction. "You're absolutely right," she said. "We do have evidence from our RBCTs, so why don't we start thinking about how we can use them to share the successes that you all have been having in your coaching work? I'll talk with the superintendent about this and make sure that you guys are on the agenda for the next board meeting." Shayla's take-charge approach had a noticeable effect on the group, and they spent the rest of their meeting that day crafting a plan for what they would present. Over the next few weeks, the coaches pulled data from their RBCTs from the past few years. Based on the game plan they had developed, they compiled the following information:

- The average number of students who met the goal of the coaching cycles

- Examples of plans that were made for follow-up with students who had not yet met the goal

- A chart showing the various areas where teachers reported having changed their teaching practice as a result of coaching, with percentages of responses for each one

- Inspiring anecdotal reflections from teachers about the changes they have seen in their students after participating in a coaching cycle

When the night arrived to present, the coaches were ready to go. With Shayla by their side, they gave a thorough and compelling presentation of the evidence, clearly demonstrating the impact their coaching has made on both student and teacher learning throughout the district. The board members had a few follow-up questions but mostly expressed how pleased they were with the work the group was doing and congratulated them on their successes. One board member even said that if the coaching program were to continue in the district, she hoped that the coaches would do a similar presentation next year.

When the budget was approved several weeks later, the coaches were relieved to find out that they had escaped the cuts and were going to be fully funded again in the coming year. Though it had been scary and upsetting to go through, they also found that aggregating all of the data was an incredibly valuable process. Each coach had known individually that they were making an impact, but having to pull it all together to demonstrate their success as a team gave them a renewed sense of confidence and excitement about their work. As for the board member's request, they made a similar presentation the following year, and that was the last they ever heard about the coaching program being on the chopping block.

Tools and Techniques

As we discussed previously, the RBCT can provide a wealth of information about the impact of our coaching. When we come together to learn and support each other, this evidence can be used for personal reflection, to give one another feedback, and to help us continue to grow. Figure 3.4 offers a protocol to guide coaches in using the RBCT in these discussions.

While it is clear that there is a tremendous value and need to measure our impact, taking the time to do things like pre-assess students, use the RBCT, or participate in exit interviews can seem like a waste of time for teachers. It is important for teachers to understand the purpose of doing these things. Language to help us navigate instances in which they express concerns is shown in Figure 3.5. The if/then charts at the end of each chapter can also be found in Resource A in this book.

FIGURE 3.4   Consultancies to Share Our Coaching Work

1. **Present the Coaching Cycle (5 minutes)**
   - Provide background about the relationship with the teacher and how the cycle got started.
   - Share the goal and learning targets for the coaching cycle.

2. **Pose Clarifying Questions (5 minutes)**
   - Ask clarifying questions to gain more understanding and context. Save probing questions for later.

3. **Examine the Results-Based Coaching Tool for the Cycle (5 minutes)**
   - Read the RBCT, and take notes. While doing so, consider whether it is "in tune" with the goal that the coach had for the cycle.

4. **Provide Strengths-Based Feedback (8 minutes)**
   - Ask probing questions and provide strengths-based feedback. This involves clarifying, valuing, and uncovering possibilities.

5. **Reflect (5 minutes)**
   - The presenter shares what was learned from the process. Other participants connect the process to their own work.

Source: Adapted from McDonald (2017).

FIGURE 3.5   Language and Strategies for Measuring the Impact of Coaching

IF I HEAR OR NOTICE . . .	THEN I CAN SAY OR DO . . .
"I don't see the value in pre-assessing the students. I already know they don't know this material, so it would just be frustrating for them and a waste of time for me."	"Using pre- and post-assessment data that is descriptive and paints a picture of how students grew across a cycle gives us tangible evidence of the impact of our coaching work. For this reason, we don't simply give the end-of-unit test at the beginning of the unit. Rather, we try to get a more nuanced view of what the students already know in relation to the success criteria. The best way to do this is through an open-ended formative assessment."
"I feel like I know my students really well, and I can tell when they get something and when they don't. It feels like a lot of extra work to constantly have to be looking at all their work if it's just going to tell me what I already know."	"You really do have an amazing sense about your students. With so much happening each day, it can be really helpful to actually look at their work or anecdotal evidence so we are crystal clear about who is doing what. The key is to make sure we're formatively assessing so we can have a really accurate picture of where each student is and what they need next in their learning."

IF I HEAR OR NOTICE . . .	THEN I CAN SAY OR DO . . .
A coach expresses concern to her teammates that using the Results-Based Coaching Tool (RBCT) will feel too cumbersome to teachers and may make them avoid wanting to do coaching cycles.	A fellow coach can reply, "We need to help teachers see that documenting our work with the RBCT is not just about filling out a form but rather it's a way to help us stay focused on the goal for student learning throughout the coaching cycle and to measure student growth from beginning to end. Not every teacher may want to have the tool present in our daily collaboration, but if it's a shared online document, then they can choose whether to access it or not."

A Final Thought

In the past several years, there has been a sense of urgency permeating our schools. We simply don't have time to waste in providing students with high-quality learning experiences that will help them become proficient readers, writers, scientists, historians, mathematicians, and thinkers. For this reason, John Hattie is spot on when he says we must "know thy impact."

As coaches we need to operate with this same sense of urgency. It is no longer okay to judge our success simply on whether or not teachers like us or find us to be helpful. We need clear data, both quantitative and qualitative, to let us know the impact we are having on student and teacher learning. We can then use this data to monitor and adjust our coaching when needed. Having clear goals for student learning, pre- and post-assessing, and using ongoing formative assessment all help us understand the impact our work is having. When we pull it all together and document our work with the RBCT, we are able to leverage this information in a variety of ways as we continue to strive to provide the most effective coaching support possible.

Student-Centered Coaching Conversations

4

Diane's daughter Eva had been taking guitar lessons from a teacher named Nick for a few years. During this time they had become friends. Now that Nick was entering his thirties, he was wondering where to go next in his career. While he loved teaching guitar, he wasn't sure if it was what he wanted to do forever. He reached out to Diane to see if she would meet with him to discuss some of his ideas. They sat down at a coffee shop on a late summer day to discuss his future.

Nick began by sharing that he most enjoyed his relationships with his teen students. He had earned a master's degree in education, but since he'd been teaching in a private music school, he wondered if he could achieve this level of connection in a more traditional school setting. He threw out the idea of pursuing a degree in counseling and also shared that he loved to travel and inquired about teaching overseas.

As he thought aloud, Diane could see so many possibilities for him. She could see him as an educator in an international school, and she could see him continuing teaching music. But she felt most strongly about his idea of pursuing a career as a counselor for teens. She had seen how easily he connected with Eva not only when it came to playing the guitar but also about the challenges of growing up as a teenager. Diane offered to put him in touch with some friends in the field, and they discussed degree programs that would best fit his needs. As they said their goodbyes, she saw this as the perfect fit for Nick and was sure that it was the path he would take.

A few months later Nick shared that he had decided to continue teaching music. Additional schooling meant debt and time, and he wasn't sure if it felt like the right fit. In a strange way Diane was disappointed to hear the news. She had latched onto the idea of Nick as a counselor and felt like it was the best choice for him. Looking back, she realized that rather than keeping an open mind and listening, she had advocated for the idea that she liked the best.

Thinking we know best isn't how most of us would define being an effective listener. It's true that we all have moments when we walk away from conversations wondering if we took over, talked too much, said the wrong thing, or failed to help our coachee construct meaning. These moments never feel good and are often at the root of our identity as a coach. Are we good listeners? Are we effective at questioning? The reality is, these skills can be practiced and improved on over time. That's what this chapter is about.

What Does Student-Centered Coaching Sound Like?

Over the years, we have refined the structures for Student-Centered Coaching. This includes defining coaching cycles, creating planning tools, and providing moves for staying focused on student learning. While these structures are essential, we recognize that we must also develop skills in the use of dialogue, habits of listening, and effective questioning. We see these behaviors as living within the structures that we create. We also see them as practices that involve continuous and lifelong work.

Ask Before Telling

Asking before telling means we enter conversations with an open stance that is driven by curiosity and the desire to understand what lies in front of us. Rather than carrying answers into conversations, we co-construct ideas together. Since learning is a process of constructing ideas, if we do too much telling, we run the risk of taking the learning away from the person we are there to coach.

Opportunities for asking before telling show up during goal setting, co-planning, when we analyze student work, and in all forms of group work. The proverb that "we were given two ears and one mouth; we should use them in that ratio" applies here. It means that, as coaches, we must be judicious with what we choose to share. This serves to not only validate the ideas of others but it increases their ownership in the decisions that are ultimately made.

Co-constructing ideas can be challenging when teachers see the coach as an expert. The risk is that we may jump in and answer questions too quickly—usually by sharing our own ideas—and undermine the voice of the teacher. Marco was a coach in a school that had adopted new reading and writing units. As the teachers implemented the units in their classrooms, they often said, "Just tell me what to do." In these moments, he went into tutorial mode. He thought that if he just explained it a little bit more clearly, they would feel more confident using the units in their classrooms. What really happened is the teachers sat passively and seemed even more confused.

One day he tried something new. When a teacher said, "I'm not sure what to do," he replied, "You know your kids best. What do you think?" Then they talked through what it would look like if the students were successful. This provided clarity around the expectations for student learning and gave them a road map to plan the next lesson. It also brought the teacher's voice into the conversation. Asking instead of telling increased the teacher's confidence and gave Marco a clear path for coaching.

Seven Norms of Collaborative Work

For many years, we have used the Seven Norms of Collaboration from Adaptive Schools (Garmston & Wellman, 2016) as a guide for our work with individuals and teams. These norms have stood the test of time because they provide a clear vision of what it means to engage in high-quality conversations. They were originally designed for group work, so they are useful tools when working with multiple people in a group cycle. They can also be helpful in individual coaching conversations. Figure 4.1 introduces how the norms fit into both aspects of a coach's work.

Crafting Conversations That Are Learning Focused

It's interesting to take a step back and ask what it means to learn. This is a broad question that applies not only to our students but to us as well. We know that learning is more successful when we are able to build on what's working rather than trying to plug holes with what's not. For this reason, we take the stance that learning is a fluid process in which we

FIGURE 4.1 Seven Norms of Collaboration

1. Pausing	
Pausing before responding allows time for thinking and enhances dialogue, discussion, and decision-making.	*In Group Cycles or Other Collaborative Work:* Group members engage thoughtfully in conversations by taking the time to think and reflect before responding. This requires us to slow down, listen, and weigh the thoughts of others before sharing our own thinking. To promote this behavior, the facilitator uses practices such as reflective writing or journaling at specific points in the conversation. Protocols that build in time for each person to contribute can also be used. This reminds us to resist the temptation to solve a problem before hearing from every group member. *In Individual Coaching Conversations:* Coaches listen attentively to the teacher before responding with their own thinking. They also recognize that coaching is more meaningful when both the teacher and coach are provided with the opportunity to build and share their knowledge and ideas over time, such as through coaching cycles.
2. Paraphrasing	
Paraphrasing allows us to hear and understand each other as we evolve in our thinking. It is used both as a means of gaining clarity and validating the thinking of others.	*In Group Cycles or Other Collaborative Work:* When a lack of clarity exists about what is being shared by a colleague, participants regularly paraphrase and seek confirmation that the message is being understood. Language for paraphrasing includes "I think what I'm hearing you say is . . ." or "It sounds like you are saying . . ." *In Individual Coaching Conversations:* Paraphrasing readily applies to coaching conversations. Using similar language, the coach paraphrases what was shared to confirm that the teacher was understood. This also serves to validate the ideas of the teachers and provides the opportunity for the coach to connect to what's already there.
3. Posing Questions Using gentle, open-ended probes or inquiries increases clarity and precision of a person's thinking.	*In Group Cycles or Other Collaborative Work:* Group members regularly question one another to enhance the overall learning of the group. Questioning is honest and open minded and has the sole purpose of clarifying and enhancing the work of the group. Examples of questions include "Can you tell me about . . . ?" or "Then, are you saying . . . ?" *In Individual Coaching Conversations:* When used effectively, questioning is a nonthreatening process that deepens and extends the learning of both the teacher and coach. Language includes "Why do we think the students responded in this way?" "What can we learn from the student work to enhance our thinking?" "I'd love to hear your thoughts on this; can you tell more?"
4. Putting Ideas on the Table Sharing ideas are the heart of meaningful dialogue. However, one	*In Group Cycles or Other Collaborative Work:* Group members understand that there are many solutions to any given problem and are encouraged to put ideas on the table throughout conversations. The ideas that are shared are invitational and open ended. Examples are "What if . . . ?" or "One thought I have is . . ." or "I'm just thinking out loud . . ."

must remain open minded and thoughtful in relation to the ideas that are being shared by oneself and others.	*In Individual Coaching Conversations:* In order to validate and learn from teachers, coaches begin most conversations by soliciting ideas from the teacher before sharing their own. Later in the conversation, a coach may share an idea or two using language, such as "One thing that might make sense is . . ." or "What do you think about . . .?" These ideas are shared in an invitational manner so the teacher maintains ownership in the decision-making.
5. Providing Data Using evidence drives the conversation toward a place of specificity. It also ensures that the focus is on student learning.	*In Group Cycles or Other Collaborative Work:* In group coaching cycles, PLCs, and data teams, various forms of evidence are used to assess student growth over time. This is done through a facilitated process that identifies where students are in relation to where they need to be. *In Individual Coaching Conversations:* The coach and teacher use student evidence as they engage in sorting sessions. This practice anchors co-planning and is driven by an ethic of continuous formative assessment.
6. Paying Attention to Self and Others Meaningful dialogue is facilitated when we are aware of both what we are saying as well as how others are responding to what is being said.	*In Group Cycles or Other Collaborative Work:* Group members demonstrate this norm by staying conscious of how their behavior affects the group. Examples include monitoring for group members who speak too often or not enough. By making a group aware of this norm, participants learn to adapt their behavior accordingly. *In Individual Coaching Conversations:* Coaching conversations, like all conversations, are a back-and-forth dialogue in which we listen, respond, and adapt to one another. By paying attention to self and others, the coach adjusts throughout the conversation and may do so by drawing upon other norms, including pausing, posing questions, and paraphrasing.
7. Presuming Positive Intentions Assuming that a colleague's comments, questions, or statements are coming from a positive place promotes and facilitates productive dialogue and eliminates unintentional resentment, hurt feelings, and misunderstandings.	*In Group Cycles or Other Collaborative Work:* Though group members may disagree with a colleague, the underlying sentiment is that they believe that the intentions of that person are positive. Groups that don't demonstrate this norm bring judgments and negative viewpoints of their colleagues into group dialogue. Groups that demonstrate this norm may use the following language: "I appreciate what you are saying . . ." "What you are saying makes sense because . . ." *In Individual Coaching Conversations:* Coaching is driven by respectful and trusting relationships, and if a coach carries a negative view of a teacher, it shows. Coaches who demonstrate this norm are open minded about both the teachers with whom they collaborate as well as how any given problem might be solved.

Source: Adapted from Garmston & Wellman (2016).

support teachers to reflect on what's working and then co-construct a plan to take the learning to the next level. What follows are a variety of strategies to help get us there.

Use Learning Targets to Build Clarity

Without learning targets, or a clear success criteria, our conversations run the risk of becoming unfocused. With learning targets, our conversations are clear and objective because they are rooted in specific outcomes for student learning.

Let's return to Marco's work with the reading and writing units. As a step toward implementation, the district sent the coaching team to attend professional development in another city. The expectation was to return and "roll out" what they learned to others. This meant that they would now be the experts and that it was their job to convey this expertise to the teachers in their schools.

The challenge became how to create the conditions for teachers to use the materials in a way that would best serve their students. One way Marco accomplished this was by working with teachers to unpack their units to a high degree of clarity instead of "downloading" the unit onto teachers. By setting up outcomes for the students' learning first, and then figuring out how to get there, he was able to do meaningful work with the units in a way that was also student-centered.

Encourage Reflection and Metacognition by Teachers

With so many initiatives, programs, and mandates in today's schools, it's a wonder we can find time for reflective thinking. Teachers are so busy that some have even resorted to taking a "divide and conquer" approach to planning. When everything is moving so fast, it can be hard to ask teachers to slow down and reflect. They may feel like they honestly don't have time for it. For this reason, it's our job to create a space for reflection in each and every conversation. It also means we may have to communicate that working with a coach is a reflective process that requires us to slow down when engaging in a coaching cycle.

Reflection is a form of metacognition, or "thinking about our thinking." This is the stance we take throughout a coaching cycle. Thinking together in this way leads us to unpack our decisions together. As Marco became more comfortable thinking alongside the teachers in his school, he was able to practice increasing metacognition throughout his coaching conversations. For example, he began a recent co-planning conversation with Sheila by asking, "What did we notice about how the students connected the characters' actions with the theme of the book?" Earlier he would have thought this question may have felt loaded, but since this was one of the learning targets that they had co-created, he knew that Sheila had been formatively assessing for this very thing. She said she noticed a disconnect with some of the books that the students were reading and explained that while she believed in providing choice to her students, a few were reading books without strong characters so when she conferred with them, the conversations remained at the surface level. She said, "It almost felt forced." Marco led Sheila toward deeper levels of metacognition by saying, "That's an important observation. As we think about this, what do we think might be the right move for tomorrow?" Sheila thought aloud with, "What if I look through their book bins after school to see what they've selected. Then we can create a small group with the students who need it?" While Marco was glad that Sheila was thinking proactively, he saw this as an opportunity for her to *think about her thinking*. He said, "That's a good idea. I wonder if it's possible to tackle this in a way that promotes student ownership. Do we think they could do some of this work themselves?" Sheila paused and asked, "What would that look like?" Marco replied, "What if we provided them with a criteria to decide if they've selected a book that matches the work we are doing with character?" Sheila said, "I like how that would put them in the driver's seat." They spent the next ten minutes constructing questions that the students could use to reflect on their book selection. It included the questions (1) Does my book have at least one character that I know very well? (2) Does the author share the characters' feelings in a way that's clear to me? and (3) Can I infer about the characters' actions?

As is usually the case, Sheila's first idea was strong. But it became stronger with additional reflection. By serving as her thinking partner, Marco probed at the right time so that she could take a step back and examine her idea, leading her to reflect in ways that will increase the outcomes for her students.

Posing questions is an effective way to promote reflection. These stems can be useful in a variety of situations:

- What would need to happen in order for . . . ?

- What would it look like if students were successful at . . . ?

- How might students show us they understand how to . . . ?

- Why is it important for students to be able to . . . ?

Providing Strengths-Based Feedback

Strengths-based feedback is feedback that respects and builds on the ideas of others. It allows us to engage with teachers in a way that honors the work they're doing while helping them grow as learners. We refer to this as "windshield feedback" because it is about looking forward rather than in the rearview mirror.

More traditional approaches to providing feedback involve practices such as naming what we saw teachers doing and then helping them to see how they could have done it differently—neither of which falls into what we would describe as being student-centered or outcomes based. Strengths-based feedback isn't an event, or single conversation. It is continuous, learning focused, productive, and respectful. It involves the following steps and is inspired by the notion of "reflective feedback" (Cheliotes & Reilly, 2010, p. 67).

1. **Clarify** to understand the whole picture.

2. **Value** what is already working.

3. **Uncover possibilities** for what might come next.

Using this structure aligns with recent research on feedback that emphasizes focusing on refining what is already there rather than trying to add something that's not (Buckingham & Goodall, 2019). This is validated by brain science that has identified the fact that we grow more neurons and synaptic connections in the places where we already have them. This means that we learn best when we build on (vs. replace) what's there. Compare this to feedback that identifies and tries to "fix" what is broken. The honest truth is we don't learn as much from these more traditional forms of feedback because "telling people how we think they should improve actually *hinders* learning" (Buckingham & Goodall, 2019).

A key component for providing strengths-based feedback is high-quality dialogue and discourse. This means we leverage skills such as questioning and listening to build on the ideas of others. While learning to do this may take some practice, it is quite freeing because as the provider of feedback, we no longer need to have the right answer all the time. Instead, the thinking is co-constructed and the ownership shifts to the coachee. When the ownership shifts, so does the likelihood that the ideas will be transferred into everyday practice.

Clarify to Understand the Full Picture

When we clarify, we listen and seek to understand what the teacher is thinking, how the students are performing, what has happened already, and what the teacher is hoping to accomplish next. The coach acts as a listener and gathers information through a process of authentic questioning. As this stage unfolds, the coach identifies what matters to the teacher and, if possible, uses student evidence to build an understanding of the students' needs. If we skip this part of the process, then we run the risk of making assumptions. By clarifying, we are able to avoid these pitfalls.

Since the coach is gathering information, clarifying mostly involves asking questions to fully understand the bigger picture. We rely upon clarifying questions because they help us gather information and are straightforward and easy to answer. Figure 4.2 provides examples of clarifying questions.

FIGURE 4.2 Examples of Clarifying Questions

- What can we see in the student work to understand how they are doing in relation to the learning targets?
- How do we feel about what we've tried already?
- How does this connect to the curricular materials or standards?

The Importance of Valuing

Teachers are under a lot of pressure. Sending the message that "I see your hard work," "I see your commitment," and "I see what you value" is vitally important. This is one reason we include valuing in the process for providing feedback. Valuing matters because it signals that the coach is listening, is aware of what's working, and is planning to build on it. There is a myth, which is debunked by brain science, that any form of praise is bad. This theory implies that we should refrain from valuing, when in truth, naming what's already there not only respects the teacher but eases their stress and motivates them to go further.

Speaking of pressure, feedback has traditionally felt like a high-stakes experience for teachers—especially because it is so often connected to an evaluation. Sitting down with a coach, and waiting for the shoe to drop via feedback can be incredibly stressful. One of the most visceral experiences of this for Diane came in the form of "critiques" when she was an art major in college. The thinking when it came to feedback was the harsher, the better. Let's just say that Diane didn't stay an art major for long. Today, some companies still subscribe to this philosophy with 360 reviews and other forms of tough love feedback. Coaches don't have to go down that road. We can reframe feedback as a positive experience, and one way we achieve this is through valuing.

Figure 4.3 provides language stems for valuing. It's important to keep in mind that this part of the process is meant to directly connect to the clarifying that has already occurred. While we are providing examples of language stems, it's best when this part of the conversation evolves naturally.

FIGURE 4.3   Language Stems for Valuing

- It looks like the students really responded to . . .
- You've been working hard on . . .
- Have you thought about sharing what we are doing with your colleagues?
- Now that's something to celebrate!

Uncovering Possibilities

The last stage for providing strengths-based feedback is uncovering possibilities. We use this language because it implies an openness and no right answer. As the coach and teacher reflect on what they have already tried and have taken a moment to celebrate, it is natural to begin envisioning what might come next. This is the moment when a coach has the opportunity to increase the teacher's metacognition. It may be as simple as thinking about how to provide students with more choice, it may be focused on how to increase student engagement or improve classroom behavior, or it may be about how students will be assessed. Whatever it is, it's co-constructed so that the ownership rests with the teacher. In this way we avoid doing it to teachers but instead do it with them.

Next steps are co-constructed in a way that sends the signal that the coach has the teacher's back. It may feel more like a planning conversation where in the past, feedback has felt like a "post observation." Taking this stance increases the potential of feedback because our goal is to create learning opportunities from every conversation we have with teachers, and the process of uncovering possibilities gets us there. Figure 4.4 provides examples of the language we use when uncovering possibilities.

FIGURE 4.4   Language Stems for Uncovering Possibilities

- What are some possibilities for . . . ?
- How can we apply this to other situations?
- What are some ways we could . . . ?
- What would it look like if we tried . . . ?

Strengths-Based Feedback Within Coaching Cycles

When providing feedback is a process rather than as a single event, it begins to tuck into each and every conversation that we have as coaches. This includes all stages of a coaching cycle. Seeing feedback in this way means we move away from viewing feedback as some kind of critique and instead view it as a generative process where ideas are explored, refined, and then acted upon. We can't stress enough that this is a new way to think about feedback, so let's unpack how feedback fits into coaching cycles (see Figure 4.5).

FIGURE 4.5   How Feedback Fits Into Coaching Cycles

Goal Setting ➡	The goal comes into focus as the coach and teacher seek to understand current student performance and uncover what the standards require. By clarifying and valuing, the coach sets a clear message that the intent is for the coaching work to align with what the teacher hopes to accomplish. Goal-setting conversations may feel messy because the process is iterative and requires the coach and teacher to build on each other's thinking. Therefore, feedback is essential.
Creating Learning Targets ➡	The construction of learning targets is a cognitively demanding conversation that requires feedback from the coach to the teacher and vice versa. As ideas are shared, we clarify and probe in order to co-construct learning targets that are aligned with the standards, are student-friendly, fit the needs of the students, and align with the curriculum.
Co-Planning and Co-Teaching ➡	Co-planning and co-teaching are rich opportunities for feedback because as we plan and teach together we are creating a shared vision for student learning. This ensures that the teacher and coach are able to teach the lesson and formatively assess student performance in real time. Our success hinges on uncovering possibilities about the intent of the lesson as well as the content and processes that will be used to facilitate student learning. Feedback is required to get there.

Questioning and Listening

By now it's probably obvious that we believe systems and structures are essential for coaching. Systems and structures scaffold us toward doing intentional work. But as we mentioned earlier, the conversations that live within the structures are also paramount. What this means is if we aren't effective in the areas of questioning and listening, then the very systems we rely upon may fall flat.

Questions ≠ Suggestions

When working with coaches, we often run into questions that are suggestions in disguise. "How about if we . . . ?" "What if you tried . . . ?" and "Do you think we could . . . ?" are all examples of ways that coaches propose different ideas to teachers by framing them in the form of questions. For example, "What if you used book clubs so that students could choose their own books?" While there is a question mark at the end of the sentence, it's really a suggestion. Thus, it shifts the conversation to the coach's ideas rather than building on the ideas of the teacher. A simple reframe would be:

"I know that you value student choice. How might we accomplish this with text selection?" This question opens the door to a deeper level of discourse because it doesn't drive toward a specific answer.

Diane recently witnessed this conversation between a teacher and coach. The coach asked her to rehearse the conversation beforehand because she was feeling frustrated and unsure about how to proceed. She thought the teacher wasn't providing students with a choice of texts—something that was being emphasized as an expected instructional practice. As they planned for the conversation, Diane wondered if the coach might begin with a clarifying question to get a better sense of the teacher's thinking. The coach agreed, and here's what happened.

> **Coach:** I know that you value student choice. How might we accomplish this with text selection?
>
> **Teacher:** I spent the summer organizing text sets so that my students could choose books based on their interests. But when I shared this idea with my team, they said that I had to stick to the reading list. I'm not sure what to do.
>
> **Coach:** Okay, how about if I help you figure out a way to use your text sets so you can stick with your beliefs about student choice? The cool thing is this aligns perfectly with the work that is happening with the ELA team.

If the coach had asked the teacher the original question she had in mind—"What if you used book clubs so that students could choose their own books?"—just think how it would have landed with the teacher. While she may have thought she understood why the teacher was making certain decisions, she would have been wrong. Asking an open-ended question led the coach to learn so much more. Here she was thinking, "She just loves assigning class novels," when this was the furthest thing from the truth.

Approaching this conversation more openly also led the teacher to feel more supported and tapped into what she was hoping to accomplish with her students. Thus, it created an opening for coaching.

The Art of Listening

Stephen Covey (2004) writes, "Most people do not listen with the intent to understand; they listen with the intent to reply" (p. 251). We can all relate to this as it is human nature to sift and sort what we are hearing in order to reply smartly. The truth is, we can guide the thinking of others just as well by listening.

We included videos of coaching conversations in *Student-Centered Coaching: The Moves* (Sweeney & Harris, 2017) because we felt that it was important to show what Student-Centered Coaching looks like in action. While the actual coaching moves we use are important, we can also pay attention to the verbal and nonverbal communication that occurs. In fact, "Nearly two-thirds of meaning between two speakers comes from nonverbal cues—what we see in the speaker's face and body, and what we hear in the voice tone" (Cheliotes & Reilly, 2010, p. 30).

Listening is an "art" because it is something that we practice continuously, much like being mindful, eating healthy, or being active. Practicing the art of listening means we are hyper aware of our behaviors, and we adjust them as needed. We've found that there is a collection of behaviors that take us away from our best listening (see Figure 4.6). The list provides a pathway to continuous improvement in the area of listening. We will provide a tool later in this chapter to guide this process.

To be honest, we see ourselves in this list. As passionate educators, we sometimes interrupt to agree or add on to what we are hearing. This sounds like "I know! I experienced this last week too!" As problem solvers,

FIGURE 4.6 Behaviors That Take Us Away From Effective Listening

- Interrupting the speaker
- Providing advice too quickly
- Thinking about our response when the speaker is still speaking
- Being uncomfortable with silence
- Piggybacking or hijacking the conversation
- Bringing our own agenda to the conversation

we sometimes provide advice too quickly, saying something like "What if you . . .?" As Stephen Covey suggests, we sometimes think about our reply as we are listening. This means we are in our own heads rather than seeking to understand what we are hearing. As type A personalities, we are at times uncomfortable with silence, even though we know that this is when the best processing occurs. As people on a mission, we piggyback or hijack the conversation, or bring our own agenda. When we do this, we take the spotlight away from the teachers and shift it to ourselves. Just like everyone else, we are working to improve our skills as listeners and will likely be doing so for the rest of our lives.

Lesson From the Field

A contractor's tools include drills, wrenches, and a hammer. A skier's tools include skis, boots, and poles. A coach's tools include a clear process, great questions, and the ability to listen well. While a bit more intangible than the tools in some other professions, they are tools nonetheless.

In our work with districts, we often practice using these tools with teams of coaches. This recently occurred in a fast-growing district in the Midwest that Leanna was supporting. The task that day was to brainstorm the language the coaches could use during co-planning and co-teaching sessions. They had already studied the flow of a coaching cycle, and their next step was to uncover the language that lived within each stage. A group of coaches sat with sticky notes and jotted down their ideas. When asked to share, Sarah offered, "I would have us look at the student evidence." Another coach added, "I would get clear about what would happen during the lesson." As she listened, Leanna realized that she was hearing a lot of "I woulds . . ." so she jumped in and said, "Let's talk about the actual language we'd use rather than share what we'd talk about. What would that sound like?" Leanna wanted Sarah to know that she was on the right track—just that she could get more specific in her language. So she probed with "Let's take your example and work with it. You said, 'I would have us look at the student evidence.' Let's craft some language that gets at this idea."

Sarah then refined her thinking and said, "Do we notice any trends in the student work?" Another coach added, "How does the work compare to the learning targets?" Then another said, "Which target should we focus in on today?" As they shared their ideas, Leanna recorded each one on a sticky note. As she listened, she wondered aloud if the group might benefit from crafting some statements as well. This way it wouldn't feel like an interrogation. A few coaches shared ideas like "I noticed that the students did . . ." and "It's impressive that your students are already demonstrating mastery in a few of the learning targets." Now it was sounding more like a conversation.

Upon reflection, the coaches noted that they hadn't thought this specifically about how they used language. With Leanna's guidance, they not only practiced what they would do but they also began to think about what they would say. In this way, they began to view coaching language as a tool that could help them be more intentional throughout their coaching conversations. They spent the rest of the afternoon role-playing and crafting language as they went. Generating language for coaching in this way helped them create a valuable tool for their coaching toolbox.

Tools and Techniques

Elena Aguilar recommends that as we strive to be better listeners, we must "listen to our own listening." She writes, "One practice that I regularly engage in and that is perhaps one of the most useful is to listen to my own listening. The exercise invites you to open a window into your mind and see what it's doing" (Aguilar, 2013, p. 277). We love the notion of "opening a window into your mind" and have created the following assessment to support this process. While there are many levels in which one might self-assess their skills as a listener, Figure 4.7 gets at the behaviors mentioned earlier in this chapter. Then, Figure 4.8 drills deeper into the conversational moves we make.

Being able to facilitate and engage in productive dialogue is one of the most important skills we need to develop as coaches. Figure 4.9 introduces situations that coaches may encounter, along with ideas on how to respond in such circumstances. The if/then charts at the end of each chapter can also be found in Resource A in this book.

FIGURE 4.7   Self-Assessing Your Behaviors as a Listener

BEHAVIOR	WHEN DO I FIND MYSELF ENGAGING IN THIS BEHAVIOR?	WHAT STRATEGIES (VERBAL AND NONVERBAL) CAN I USE TO IMPROVE AS A LISTENER?
Interrupting the speaker		
Providing advice too quickly		
Thinking about my response while the speaker is still speaking		
Being uncomfortable with silence		
Piggybacking or hijacking the conversation		
Bringing my own agenda to the conversation		

online resources ⬉ Available for download at **resources.corwin.com/EssentialGuideforSCCoaching**

FIGURE 4.8   Self-Assessing Your Behaviors at the Conversational Level

1. What kinds of questions do I ask? Clarifying, probing, other?

2. What nonverbal cues do I send that I'm listening? How do I take notes at the same time?

3. How did I feel during silence or "think time"?

4. How many suggestions did I make? And how much did I build on the ideas of others?

FIGURE 4.9 Language and Strategies for Student-Centered Conversations

IF I HEAR OR NOTICE . . .	THEN I CAN SAY OR DO . . .
A grade-level team meets weekly to co-plan as part of their coaching cycle. Certain group members dominate the conversation. Their focus is on efficiency, and it seems like they don't want to take time for everyone to reflect as part of the learning process.	It's the facilitator's role to ensure that in collaborative conversations, groups are balanced and productive. In this case, the coach may lead the group to unpack the Seven Norms of Collaboration to uncover what it would look and feel like to put the norms into practice. At the end of each session, the group then uses the norms to reflect on the quality of their conversation and then set a goal for how they might continue to improve.
A coach and teacher are co-planning together. The teacher turns to the coach and says, "Since you know the curriculum, it would be great if you planned the lesson. Then you can just tell me what you want me to do."	The coach responds by saying, "I appreciate that, but you know your kids the best. How about if we start by doing a quick sort of your student work, and then we can sketch out the lesson together. This way, we'll both be able to think about the students and the curriculum at the same time. How does that sound?"
A teacher shares that the principal has been providing lots of feedback through the formal evaluation process. The teacher says, "I feel pretty good about it and don't really think I need to work with a coach."	The coach explains, "The feedback that you received as part of the evaluation process is completely different from what happens in Student-Centered Coaching. Rather than feeling like it is being done to you, coaching is a partnership that's about helping your students meet the goals you set for them."

A Final Thought

The metacognitive lift of coaching is not to be underestimated. We are simultaneously thinking about the coaching process, the content, the language we use, and how to listen . . . all at the same time. For this reason, the strategies and ideas presented in this chapter are about continuous learning.

It never feels good to walk away from a conversation wondering if you said too much, hijacked it, or felt like you and the teachers weren't on the same page. Even with the strongest and most trusting relationships, these feelings can surface, and when they do, it leads us to wonder if we added to (or took away from) the learning of others. To this day Diane wonders if she was too strident in her conversation with Nick. Of course, he is an adult who will make his own decisions, but she wanted to be sure that he got what he was looking for, a person to truly listen to him on that day in the coffee shop.

Building a Culture Where Student-Centered Coaching Thrives

5

//

Diane wondered what might greet her as she parked her car in front of a high school in Denver. Through a grant, she had been hired as a visiting coach in the school. When the project began, the principal had e-mailed to let her know that she would be working with the science department. So far, they had met a few times, and it had been rocky. She was hoping that today would be a turning point.

On her previous visit, Diane worked with the team to set the following goal for the coaching cycle: *Students will analyze data from investigations and use mathematical thinking to describe the energy changes both quantitatively and conceptually.* After unpacking the goal, they created a pre-assessment that would surface what the students already knew about data analysis and energy. As a science-focused charter school, the assumption was that a portion of the students would already have an understanding of some aspects of the content. They would use this evidence to plan the lessons that they would co-teach later in the day.

When Diane entered the conference room that morning, she found the three teachers already seated. She began by asking how it went with the pre-assessment. There was a moment of hesitation, and then one of the teachers shared that they never gave it. "It seemed like a waste of time," he explained. The other two teachers nodded sheepishly and looked away. Diane wasn't sure what to say, and even more importantly, she wondered what evidence they would use to co-plan. As if he read her mind, the teacher added, "We have our lessons already planned, so if you want to help out in our classes, that would be fine." With that, the door to coaching was closed.

Coaching in a school that is prepared to engage is an entirely different experience. More recently, Diane worked with a team of coaches in another Denver school. On a winter afternoon, she observed a first-grade teacher and coach analyzing student work from earlier in the day. As Emily and Jennifer worked through the stack of student writing, they began to run short on time. They knew the bell was about to ring and didn't want to miss this chance to collaborate, so a colleague who was sitting nearby said, "I'll get your kids so you can finish up your coaching session." With these few extra minutes, the teacher and coach were able to analyze the writing and plan the next lesson. This "get the job done" attitude is a sure sign that they valued coaching.

Each of these examples illustrates the role culture plays in how teachers respond to coaching. Rather than being the victim of a culture that already exists, it is essential for schools to take intentional steps to prepare the culture for coaching.

Crafting a culture that makes the most out of coaching is guided by the school leader. In the first example, the principal received resources to bring in Diane as a visiting coach. Rather than building a plan with the teachers, she told them they would get coached. She took a hands-off approach and expected that with a few weeks of coaching, Diane would be able to get the team up to speed and scores would improve. Coaching was being done *to* them instead of *with* them. No wonder they didn't feel like engaging.

In the second example, the principal developed a team of teacher leaders who worked with her to create a plan for coaching in the school. They studied a variety of coaching models and chose Student-Centered Coaching. Then they worked in teams to pave the way for the work. By the time that Diane arrived, everyone knew why coaching mattered. The school had been prepared for coaching, and as a result, coaching took root.

Fostering a Culture of Learning

Organizations operate within a given culture. This is clear when you visit an Apple Store. Everyone in the store looks as though they belong in an alternative rock band or posing in a fashion magazine. Techno music pumps ough the store, and there is a youthful and cutting-edge vibe. Do you suppose the Apple culture is an accident? Not a chance. It has been carefully designed and cultivated and has been pivotal to the company's success.

The culture in schools is also a key ingredient for success, and we could stand to learn a lot from organizations like Apple as we often underestimate our role in crafting a culture that fosters learning. According to Robert Evans (1996), "A careful look at the true nature of culture and functions of organizational culture reveals that it operates at a profound level, exerting a potent influence over beliefs and behavior to preserve continuity and oppose change" (p. 41).

Having worked in many schools, we have learned that schools with a culture of learning engage in the behaviors described in Figure 5.1. Thus, as we move through this chapter, we will unpack each of these characteristics in relation to the implementation of Student-Centered Coaching. In doing so, we hope to provide a clear vision for how to prepare your school culture to get the most out of a coaching effort.

FIGURE 5.1   Characteristics of Schools With a Culture of Learning

- Embrace the mess of learning, with every member of the community taking the stance of learner.
- Use student evidence and data to drive decision-making.
- Reflect on and adjust teaching practices based on the needs of students.
- Use shared decision-making so that teachers' voices, experiences, and perspectives are taken into account.
- Focus school improvement efforts on a single goal or strategy.

Embrace the Mess of Learning, With Every Member of the Community Taking the Stance of Learner

Risk is unavoidable if we are going to embark on a learning path. Learners have to, as Roland Barth (2007) puts it, "risk disclosing to the world that they don't know how and that they intend to learn how" (p. 214). This includes coaches, who often feel that they're expected to have all the answers and can feel vulnerable when they don't. When asking others to stare down the risk, fear, and discomfort that is associated with new learning, we can create an island of safety within a sea of change. Remembering that every adult learner is different (much like the students in our classrooms), we can create scaffolds that ease them into learning gracefully. If we expect and embrace the mess of adult and student learning, then we will set the stage for professional growth. This is one of the reasons why coaching is so important in today's schools. We are not only trying to meet the needs of a diverse array of learners but are trying to do so while under enormous pressure.

Make Our Learning Visible

Michael Fullan (2001) reminds us that change takes time and effort, especially when changing a school's culture: "It is no doubt clear by now why there can never be a recipe or cookbook for change, nor a step-by-step process. Reculturing is a contact sport that involves hard, labor-intensive work. It takes time and indeed never ends" (p. xvii). If we hope to create the conditions where students are learning, then all members of the school community had better get comfortable putting their own learning out there.

Making our learning visible means we ask questions, name challenges, and settle into the role of adult learner. Those who have coached for some time have likely experienced the authenticity and richness of conversations when both participants are truly grappling, wondering, and making meaning together. These are the conversations we seek.

The notion of making our learning visible isn't limited to teachers. At an elementary school in Washington, Principal Hawkins Cramer was leading his school through a four-year shift in how they taught literacy and math. As the lead learner in the school, he made his learning visible by trying his own hand at teaching lessons from the new curriculum. He'll tell you that a few of his lessons went very well (a good learning experience) and others were flops (an even better learning experience). But what really mattered is that by making his learning visible, he sent the message that this work would involve taking risks in order to grow.

Build Trust

Establishing trust is something that we can't neglect for the simple reason that teaching is incredibly hard work. According to the US Department of

Education, over 50 percent of new teachers leave the profession within the first five years, and teachers with fewer than ten years of experience constitute over 52 percent of the teaching force. If we hope to have any chance of retaining teachers, then we must learn how to create supportive environments where teachers can dig in and do the hard work together. Otherwise, they will be isolated and overwhelmed, and they may choose to leave teaching behind.

Tschannen-Moran (2004) defines trust as "the willingness to be vulnerable to another based on the confidence that the other is benevolent, honest, open, reliable, and competent" (p. 17). When any of these elements are missing, it can be difficult to create a trusting community. One of the ways a coach builds trust is to frame coaching through the lens of student learning. This orientation is *benevolent* because student learning is why teachers show up every day, and it's why students come to school in the first place. It is *honest* as long as we hold fast on using a student-centered approach and avoid slipping into coaching that is oriented around making teachers do things that may, or may not, address the needs of their students. It is *open* when the coach uses techniques such as effective listening and questioning. It is *reliable* when coaches create systems for coaching cycles and stick with them through all of the predictable interruptions throughout the school year. It is *competent* when teachers feel that the coach is both skillful and knowledgeable.

We are asking a lot from teachers when we introduce coaching into a school. If trust is missing, many will close the door to the classroom and avoid it, much like the science team that Diane coached. Bryk and Schneider (2003) found this to be true in their research of over 400 schools in Chicago. They write, "Talking honestly with colleagues about what's working and what's not means exposing your own ignorance and making yourself vulnerable. Without trust, genuine conversations of this sort remain unlikely" (p. 40). Since we know that honest conversations are at the heart of coaching, we must create the conditions for teachers to authentically engage in coaching.

Culture and Confidentiality

We are regularly asked about the role of confidentiality in relation to coaching. It is a question that hearkens back to when coaching was directed at teachers who were considered to be struggling. The fear was that if we didn't keep coaching private, trust would be broken and teachers wouldn't engage. This makes a whole lot of sense when coaching is about fixing teachers. After all, when it is driven by a deficit perspective, who would want their participation to be broadcast throughout the school?

When taking a student-centered approach, there is no need to maintain confidentiality. In fact, the opposite is true. We find that there is power in celebrating who is participating and how their participation is supporting the students to learn and grow. Later in this chapter you will meet Katie, a coach in South Carolina. Katie started her coaching cycles with the strongest teachers in the school and made sure everyone knew it. In this way, she was able to frame coaching as being for everyone, which created collective teacher efficacy throughout the school.

As we discuss confidentiality, it's important to consider the importance of coaches maintaining a high degree of professionalism when working with teachers. This means we respect the learning process, we are fair, we don't gossip or share in inappropriate ways, and we don't take sides in the inevitable drama that we find in schools. A coach must be trustworthy to all. We recommend the following norms for sharing the work that is occurring in a way that builds, rather than erodes, trust among teachers (see Figure 5.2).

FIGURE 5.2   Norms for Sharing Our Coaching Work

- The principal and coach take an asset-based perspective when discussing teachers.
- Discussions about coaching are framed through the lens of what the students are doing as learners.
- The principal spends time in classrooms so that the coach isn't put in the position to report on issues related to teacher performance.
- The principal defines clear expectations for instructional practice so that the coach doesn't have to.
- The principal defines expectations for teacher engagement in coaching cycles.
- Teachers understand that what they are focusing on in a coaching cycle will be shared with the principal unless the teacher indicates the desire not to share this information.
- Teachers understand that growth across coaching cycles will be documented and shared using the Results-Based Coaching Tool (RBCT).

Use Student Evidence and Data to Drive Decision-Making

Another way to create a culture of learning is to integrate student evidence into existing collaborative structures, such as within coaching cycles, PLCs, informal planning conversations, data teams, etc. When collaboration is driven by student evidence, coaching feels less judgmental. As a result, trust and buy-in increase. Asking questions like "What did we notice about how the students tackled the problem?" or "What trends are we seeing in the student work?" are less evaluative and lead us towards making better decisions for our students.

"Let's Look at the Student Work"

Recently, Diane was working with a coach and teacher as they discussed a co-teaching session. Corey, the coach, began the conversation by asking the teacher how she thought the lesson went. The teacher responded, "It was okay. I liked how the students discussed the text." Then she went on to talk about the things she thought she should have done better. Meanwhile, they had collected student evidence that included annotations of two texts and observational data during the student discussions. A subtle, but powerful, shift would have been to begin with the student work rather than with how the teacher felt about the lesson. Starting with "Let's look at the annotations" roots the conversation in the student learning and opens the door to a specific conversation about instructional next steps. This example of how we use student evidence demonstrates the difference between Student-Centered Coaching and teacher-centered coaching.

A cultural shift happens when schools integrate student evidence into professional conversations. Analyzing responses to reading, entrance and exit slips, student reflections on their learning, anecdotal notes, conference notes, running records, or any other student work leads teachers to form a deeper understanding of where students are and where they need to be. This anchors each and every coaching conversation in learning.

Reflect On and Adjust Practice Based on the Needs of Students

As educators, we use the word *reflect* so often that it can begin to feel vague and undefined. Does reflection occur if we ask teachers to share their lesson plans during team meetings? Or is it rooted in dutifully following the PLC model? We've all witnessed teachers who participate in these types of professional learning conversations without a whole lot of reflection taking place.

When reflection rests on a foundation of formative assessment, then we become student-centered in our decision-making. This means we reflect upon (1) what the students know, (2) what the learning targets or success criteria deems they need to know, and (3) how to design and implement instruction that meets these needs. Achieving this is a complex process that requires the following knowledge:

- Teachers understand how to apply a variety of methods, techniques, and strategies to formatively assess students throughout their learning.

- Teachers have a well-developed knowledge of the standards and curriculum they teach.

- Teachers draw from a deep well of instructional strategies and practices to promote student learning.

As you read through these behaviors, you may notice that they define the art of teaching, and it may feel like a lot. The good news is that we can get there by providing high-quality professional learning and coaching cycles. Will it take time? Of course. But knowing that this is what we are aiming for only makes high-quality coaching and collaboration that much more important.

Formative Assessment as a Driver of Student-Centered Coaching

Formative assessment is a core component of Student-Centered Coaching because it helps teachers understand how to use student evidence to drive their decision making and meet the students' needs. In their seminal work on formative assessment in the mid-1990s, Black and Wiliam (1998) write, "In order to serve a formative function, an assessment must yield evidence that, with appropriate construct-referenced interpretations, indicates the existence of a gap between actual and desired levels of performance, and suggests actions that are in fact successful in closing the gap." James Popham (2008) concurs and defines *formative assessment* as follows: "Formative assessment is a process used by teachers and students during instruction that provides feedback to adjust ongoing teaching and learning to improve students' achievement of intended instructional outcomes."

As a newly hired high school coach, Andrea wasn't sure how she would gain credibility with teachers from different subject areas. Having been a math teacher, she knew she had inroads there. But what about coaching in history, English, or world language classes?

This was on her mind when she had her first professional development session with the coaching team. Rather than giving her the green light to focus on the math department, as she had secretly hoped, it was suggested that since Student-Centered Coaching is based on the analysis of student work, she would coach across subject areas. The key is that she would be able to ask thoughtful questions and serve as a thinking partner with teachers.

The administrators who joined the meeting later in the day agreed. Their vision was for Andrea to coach across departments because they knew it would take time to build trust in the coaching program and they didn't want to "assign" coaching to the math department. They had also identified a schoolwide focus of formative assessment across grades and subjects. Their vision for coaching was for Andrea to support this rather than being a content expert in math.

This notion shifted how Andrea viewed her role as a coach. As the year progressed, she realized that she felt like a better coach when she wasn't coaching the math department. Sure, there were times when she had to study the standards and curriculum, but her administrators had been correct. Focusing on formative assessment rather than solely on content meant that coaching was relevant to all teachers.

Use Shared Decision-Making so Teachers' Voices, Experiences, and Perspectives Are Taken Into Account

In today's schools, there are countless decisions to make, and each of these decisions impact the school culture. If we hope to authentically engage teachers in coaching, then we have to make the time to hear from a broad array of voices in order to create a feeling of inclusion rather than exclusion. Making this happen means we can't neglect the voices that are present within our schools.

Build a Shared Understanding of Coaching

By now, most teachers will have had some experience with coaching. These experiences will have formed a variety of assumptions about what to expect. There may be concerns that the coach will be an arm of the administration, that hiring a coach will increase their class size, or that participating will take too much time—thinking that has the potential to build suspicion or distrust in the coaching program.

If we design coaching to involve the entire school community, then we had better hear from teachers when deciding what it will look like. This involves getting clear on what the coach's role will be, how their work will tie to existing initiatives, and how teachers will get involved.

Figure 5.3 provides questions to help a school articulate the purpose and process for coaching. In the end, it's about listening, responding, and framing a coaching model that is well understood and valued by the school community.

FIGURE 5.3   Questions for Building a Shared Understanding of Coaching

- Do teachers understand why having a coach is important? If not, how can we better articulate the value of coaching?

- Do teachers understand the beliefs and practices for the coaching model? If not, how can we help teachers to better understand what participation will look like?

- Do teachers understand how coaching will impact student learning? If not, how can we articulate this connection?

- Has the school leader solicited feedback from a broad array of teachers about coaching? If not, how can we reach out and get more teacher input?

- Has the school leader listened to teachers and adapted the plan to address any concerns they might have about coaching? If not, how can we adapt to their concerns?

- Has the school leader communicated how these concerns were taken into account in order to create the plan? If not, how can we share our process in constructing the coaching model?

Focus School Improvement Efforts on a Single Goal or Strategy

Effective schools are focused schools. Achieving the required level of focus demands clarity about the strategies or initiatives that are being used to increase student achievement during any given school year. One of the most predictable failures comes from having too many initiatives going at once. This creates a feeling of disempowerment among teachers because it's hard to be an engaged learner when you are overwhelmed.

Mike Schmoker (2019) recommends for school and district leadership to "(1) ensure that schools pursue a *severely reduced* number of initiatives and (2) select and focus on only the most urgently needed, evidence-based instructional initiatives" (p. 24). We recognize that this may be easier said than done and that while the idea of scaling back the workload sounds appealing, it can be hard to do when there is so much to accomplish. But it is well worth the effort to help create a school culture where student and teacher learning thrives.

Coaching in a Focused Environment

Coaches perform at higher levels when they work in focused schools. Conversely, we can expect that coaches will have a hard time finding their way in a school that is all over the map when it comes to improvement strategies. Imagine a school that is implementing a 1:1 technology system, reading workshop, and is rewriting the report cards all at the same time. How could a coach possibly support all of this at once?

When a school narrows the focus of professional learning, then a coach can more easily tuck that learning into coaching cycles. In Chapter 1, you read about how Joy was able to leverage a focus of providing students with time to reason and think on their own in math into her coaching cycles. Helping the math teachers understand and provide time for productive struggle was built into each lesson that she co-planned and co-taught. The best part is that Joy didn't have to introduce a whole lot of strategies for productive struggle to teachers because they were already learning about them through their professional learning as a math cohort.

Lesson From the Field

As the principal, Susan knew all too well about the importance of working in partnership with Katie, her coach. When Katie was hired to be a coach at the 750-student school, she began by building relationships with the teachers and students. As she started to learn more about coaching and reflected on what she hoped to accomplish, it became apparent that this was something she could not make happen on her own. She and Susan would need to work together to gain clarity about coaching and then leverage that shared understanding so that coaching would flourish.

As Katie started her second year as a coach, the district adopted Student-Centered Coaching as the coaching model. Susan understood that it was not only her responsibility to help Katie get her bearings with the new model but that she would have to learn how to lead the coaching effort as well. With this partnership in mind, they worked together to create a plan for how they would implement Student-Centered Coaching at her school.

Since they knew that drive-by coaching would be scattershot, Susan and Katie focused on paving the way for coaching cycles. In doing so, they were able to separate the coaching role from administrative duties such as behavior intervention and coordinating state assessments. While these tasks are important, Susan knew that if she put too much on Katie's plate, then she'd never have time for coaching cycles. They also worked together to define how their roles would overlap. This involved a discussion to uncover not only the coach's duties but the duties of the principal as well. To frame this conversation, they used a Venn diagram to allow for a discussion of how the principal and coach will work in tandem to reach their goals for the coaching program.

Even with careful planning, there were still misconceptions among the teachers about Katie's role. This was discovered when the teachers had the chance to share what they perceived was the role of the coach. They indicated that they expected a coach would provide resources and help them implement programs—both practices that aren't prioritized in Student-Centered Coaching. To respond, Susan and Katie facilitated a presentation that introduced the process. They also described how it would align with district initiatives and explained how the teachers would be provided with choice in the process. In addition to the faculty-wide conversation, Susan and Katie followed up with grade-level teams during data meetings to answer questions and address concerns. They knew that defining the role of the coach was essential and took the necessary steps to do just that.

Susan recognized that her role as the school leader was to set the tone that coaching was for everyone, not just for new teachers or those who struggle. If she didn't take this step, then teachers may opt out because they wouldn't see coaching as applying to them. To emphasize that coaching is for everyone, they used the following quote when communicating with teachers: "Teachers are scientists, working day in and day out to better understand how to help their students learn" (Sweeney & Harris, 2017). To reinforce this message, Katie's first coaching cycles were with some of the strongest teachers in the school. Later, she began working with six brand-new teachers as well as teams in more frequently assessed grade levels. Over the course of the year, she coached teachers in kindergarten, second, third, fourth, and fifth grades. Working with a variety of teachers communicated that everyone can use support in helping students grow, and Katie would be their partner in this challenging work.

Since Katie and Susan aspired to create a transparent and responsive coaching program, they recognized that coaching cycle data would be a powerful tool to not only monitor impact but also to continue to engage teachers in the process. They understood that data can sometimes be seen as threatening and evaluative, but when teachers witness student growth, it creates positive energy and purpose. They looked at their state-wide testing data to identify the curricular areas where the school had the most room for improvement and then framed these as a key area of focus for Katie's coaching cycles. This helped the teachers understand that the work they would do with Katie was targeted to what the students needed the most.

As Katie documented and shared the impact of her coaching work, enthusiasm spread like wildfire around the school. Even so, Susan and Katie recognized that word of mouth alone would not be sufficient to sustain the culture, so they took deliberate steps to celebrate the growth they were seeing, such as through a shared newsletter, as part of Susan's morning announcements, and through their school Instagram accounts. By doing this work together, Susan and Katie learned that if they understood how coaching was impacting student learning, then they could leverage this understanding to generate even more engagement among teachers. This not only prepared the school for coaching but it fostered a culture of learning as well.

Tools and Techniques

Throughout this chapter we have painted a picture of what it takes to create a school that is ready for, and benefits from, a coaching effort. Figure 5.4 provides a tool to uncover how the principal and coach roles work together to achieve this goal. By thinking about how our roles are complementary, we can get on the same page when communicating with teachers about what to expect from coaching. We also included a success criteria to serve as a road map for how to build a culture for coaching in your school in Resource C of this book.

FIGURE 5.4 Principal and Coach Self-Assessment

AS THE PRINCIPAL, I . . .		
BEHAVIOR	**SCALE 1 = LEAST OFTEN, 10 = MOST OFTEN**	**WHEN AND HOW CAN I DO MORE OF THIS?**
Keep student learning at the forefront of every conversation.	1 3 5 7 10	
Continually reinforce the purpose and practices for Student-Centered Coaching.	1 3 5 7 10	
Model and maintain a learning stance.	1 3 5 7 10	
Clearly articulate expectations regarding instructional practice.	1 3 5 7 10	
Create time in the schedule for teachers to engage in meaningful collaboration.	1 3 5 7 10	
Regularly and wholeheartedly participate in teacher collaboration.	1 3 5 7 10	
Share my own learning with others.	1 3 5 7 10	
Listen and respond to the ideas and concerns of others.	1 3 5 7 10	
Set the tone that "we are all learners" and no one has it all figured out.	1 3 5 7 10	

| AS THE COACH, I . . . | | |
BEHAVIOR	SCALE 1 = LEAST OFTEN, 10 = MOST OFTEN	WHEN AND HOW CAN I DO MORE OF THIS?
Keep student learning at the forefront of every conversation.	1 3 5 7 10	
Consistently use the practices for Student-Centered Coaching so that teachers understand what it means to engage with a coach.	1 3 5 7 10	
Build trusting and respectful relationships with all teachers.	1 3 5 7 10	
Model and maintain a learning stance.	1 3 5 7 10	
Create a system where teachers can engage in coaching cycles in the way that best suits their needs.	1 3 5 7 10	
Avoid the trap of negativity when working with teachers. Stay focused on the positive.	1 3 5 7 10	
Actively listen and respond to teachers.	1 3 5 7 10	
Celebrate student and teacher growth by documenting coaching cycles.	1 3 5 7 10	

online resources ⏷ Available for download at **resources.corwin.com/EssentialGuideforSCCoaching**

A positive, trusting school culture isn't something that can be created overnight. It comes from lots of intentional planning and messaging, and the shift can take time for everyone to get on board. Figure 5.5 provides you with useful language for building a culture that is ready for coaching. The if/then charts at the end of each chapter can also be found in Resource A in this book.

FIGURE 5.5 Language for Building a Culture That Supports Coaching

IF I HEAR . . .	THEN I CAN USE THE FOLLOWING LANGUAGE . . .
"I finally feel like I'm in a pretty good place with my teaching. I'm just not sure I want to take on all that's involved with coaching."	"Teaching is hard work, that's for sure. And it's tempting to want to maintain the status quo and catch our breath for a while. But if you're willing to embrace the messiness of learning together, I bet we can really take it to the next level with your students by building on all the great work you're already doing."
"I don't think I would feel comfortable with you telling our principal about the work you're doing in my class."	"Please know that my role is not to evaluate you or try to 'fix' you as a teacher. The idea is for us to work together to help your students learn. I would never speak with the principal about what you are or aren't doing in your classroom. Rather, I would share the different things we are trying and how your students are progressing toward meeting the goal we set for their learning."
"I have two students who have serious behavior issues and are derailing my whole class. Can you please take them to provide some targeted behavior intervention?"	"I think you'll want to take this concern to the intervention team. I'm not sure if you remember the presentation our principal and I gave during our last staff meeting, but she was explaining how coaching is going to look different this year from what we've had in the past. My role is not to provide interventions or just be a resource to teachers but to work with teachers in coaching cycles toward a goal for student learning."

A Final Thought

We used to think about coaching as a stand-alone solution for teacher learning. Then we realized how much the school culture shapes the outcome of coaching. This came to us after several experiences working with committed coaches in schools that hadn't yet developed a culture for learning. Issues around culture stymied their impact and confirmed our understanding about how important culture is if we want coaching to impact students and teachers.

This chapter uncovered the research and practices for tackling the challenging work of school culture. Learning from schools like those that have been included in this chapter provides us with clarity around how the principal and coach can build a culture that is ready for coaching.

Systems to Make Student-Centered Coaching Happen

6

One summer in middle school, Leanna's son Lorenzo decided that he wanted to run a sports camp for the younger kids in the neighborhood. Lorenzo was a true sports enthusiast, and he was always looking to make some extra spending money. Leanna applauded her son's entrepreneurial spirit but questioned whether he would be able to pull it off. Without dashing his hopes, she asked a series of questions to get him thinking about how he could make the sports camp happen: "How will you get kids to enroll?" "What would the hours be?" "How will the time be spent?" and "What do you think you should charge?" Clearly having no idea how to answer any of these questions, Lorenzo got busy making a plan.

The first thing he addressed was the structure of the camp. He wanted to offer it each week for four weeks in a nearby park. It would be Monday through Friday, from 9:00 to 12:00, and each day they would engage in two sports, starting with some skill development and then actually playing a game. Thinking about what he had access to for space and supplies, he figured they could cover soccer, baseball, football, and basketball.

Next, Lorenzo thought about how he would get kids to sign up. Given his target market was five- to nine-year-olds (being only thirteen himself), he knew that this decision would be made by the parents rather than by the kids themselves. So he asked Leanna to help by reaching out to all of her friends in the neighborhood to share an e-mail he created. Then he put up flyers at a nearby ice cream shop and personally reached out to a few parents he knew.

It started with just three kids, but over the course of the four weeks it gained momentum as word got out that the sports "camp" was actually a lot of fun. In the end, Lorenzo definitely felt like it was a success, and Leanna was proud of how her son took an idea and made it a reality. The new bike he bought with his earnings was the icing on the cake.

In Chapter 2 we explored what coaching cycles are. Now it's time to think about how to make them happen. Just as Lorenzo had to plan for how to make his sports camp idea come to life, principals and coaches need to be thoughtful about the systems and structures it will take to successfully implement Student-Centered Coaching.

Marketing and Messaging

You don't need an MBA to know that in order to sell something, it's going to take some marketing. Be it a new product, service, initiative, or business, a large part of the success will be based on how well it is explained or pitched to potential customers. In the case of Student-Centered Coaching, the customers we're trying to attract are the teachers with whom we work, and we need to help them understand what we're offering if we want them to "buy" or engage in it. This is especially relevant when making a switch from a more teacher-centered coaching model. In these cases, teachers may associate coaching with evaluation, or they may have the impression that coaching is about "fixing" in that it's just for new teachers or those who aren't very effective. When explaining what Student-Centered Coaching is, there may also be a need to do some work around helping people understand how it's different from the way things have been done in the past. In Chapter 1 we shared the dartboard that explains the difference between relationship-driven, teacher-centered, and Student-Centered Coaching and how we try to get as close to the bullseye of student learning as much as possible (see Figure 1.1). This graphic can be used as a first step in marketing Student-Centered Coaching.

Think Multiple Times and Multiple Ways

When teaching a new concept or skill, we know that students need to be exposed to it many times in order for the learning to stick. In the business world, this is known as the Rule of Seven, and it means that a potential customer needs to hear your message seven times before they buy something from you. But as Andrea Stenberg (2015) states, "The number seven isn't cast in stone. The truth of the Rule of Seven is you can't just engage in a marketing activity and then be done. Marketing must be an ongoing process in order for it to be successful." In thinking about how to get the word out about Student-Centered Coaching cycles, the natural starting point is the launch at the beginning of the year. But hearing something once won't do the job. We need to be continually looking for opportunities to get the message out. Often when we hear concerns that coaching isn't taking hold in a particular school, we find out that after the principal and coach made the initial presentation at the beginning-of-the-year faculty meeting, nothing more was said about it. With the barrage of information on new procedures, initiatives, and students, it's no wonder that such a presentation would "go in one ear and out the other" for many teachers. Messaging around coaching needs to be part of an ongoing plan if we want teachers to embrace and engage in it.

Similarly, we know we can't only use a single modality when teaching students something new. Learning happens when we process information visually, auditorily, and kinesthetically. This means we should be looking for lots of different platforms to communicate our message. A whole staff presentation could be a great place to start. But what else is there? Some coaches like to write letters to the staff that they share via e-mail. Others use digital platforms to create entertaining skit-like presentations of information such as Powtoon, or utilize other online resources for a personal website or newsletter that is blasted out to staff from time to time. Of course, there is always informal one-on-one communication that can be happening between the principal or coach and individual teachers to keep sharing the message about coaching too. While it's important to consider how to market coaching to the whole school, it can also be useful to think about a more focused approach. In a large high school with over eighty teachers and only one coach, for example, it may make sense to target a few specific departments at a time rather than messaging to a full faculty.

Just like with a new business, there is no magic bullet for marketing a coaching program. The important thing is that our efforts are ongoing and that they involve lots of different ways of communicating the message.

Start With the *Why*

Before we can get going with a variety of different platforms to share our message, we have to be thoughtful about what it is we want to share.

Teachers will need to know *what* Student-Centered Coaching is and how it's different from other types of coaching. Key messages include coaching is a partnership, it's not about fixing teachers, it's focused on goals for student learning, and it's connected to our schoolwide goals and other systems for professional learning. Then there's the structure piece: coaching happens in cycles over four to six weeks, we co-plan and co-teach every week, and we use student evidence to inform our instructional decisions.

Being explicit about what Student-Centered Coaching entails is critical to making our work successful. But if we want teachers to engage authentically rather than out of mere compliance, we have to make the case for why coaching matters. In the words of Simon Sinek (2009), if we want people to buy into what we have to offer, we first need to "start with the WHY."

Erin, a former colleague of Leanna's who teaches middle school math, takes this approach whenever she plans a new unit. Whatever the topic, she first starts by asking herself, "Why do I care about this?" Erin believes that if she can't figure out why she should care about ratios or integers or whatever else it is she's going to teach, there's no way she will get her students to care either. The same holds true for coaches. If we can't make the case for why coaching matters, why should we expect anyone else to see the value in engaging? There are no right or wrong answers to this question, and they may vary depending on each person's personal beliefs about coaching.

We believe coaching matters because:

- We are smarter together.
- Student learning is our shared purpose.
- They are OUR students.
- The job of teaching is too complex to do alone.
- We are never done getting better at our craft.
- We are all learners.
- Coaching is for everyone because it's about continual improvement.

As you think about your why, we encourage you to think boldly. This helps to create the sense that working with a coach is critical to our success as teachers, which we believe to be true. Figure 6.1 offers an example of how Kelly, a middle school coach, shared what Student-Centered Coaching is and why it matters. She used a Smore (an online newsletter) to communicate to teachers her deeply held beliefs about coaching and to define what Student-Centered Coaching is and is not.

FIGURE 6.1 Messaging Student-Centered Coaching

Coaching Update!
What's New in Coaching!?!

My Vision of Coaching

I serve teachers, students, administrators, and the community to empower them to take learning risks. Focusing on students and their learning is the best way to empower others to take risks. This is hard work, and it takes a lot of effort. Students learning is worth it.

Guiding Principles

No matter what I do, I hold myself responsible to these guiding principles:

1. Put kids first: They are the reason I am here, to help them learn.
2. Listen: I listen more than I talk. Learn about the other person or people.
3. Ask questions: Seek first to understand by asking questions.
4. Collaborate: Work with others; learn about and bring in a different perspective.
5. Act: If something should be done, do it or help do it.
6. Be positive: Look for the good in what is happening; presume positive intent.

Student-Centered Coaching Defined

Student-Centered Coaching *is*. . .

- an opportunity for me and you to work in a partnership.
- guided by learning targets based on the standards.
- deciding instructional strategies based on student evidence.

Student-Centered Coaching is *not* . . .

- evaluation.
- me telling someone what to do.
- a "fix the teacher" mentality.

Organize the Year Into Coaching Rounds

In Chapter 2 we examined how coaching cycles fit into a coach's weekly schedule, making time for co-planning and co-teaching multiple times a week with several different individuals and groups. In order to institutionalize this structure into how we operate as a school, it's also helpful to think about how coaching cycles fit within a school year.

Some coaches feel that it works best to begin and end cycles on a rolling basis as teachers seek out their support. Others find they get more traction when they organize their coaching cycles into a series of rounds over the course of the school year. Simply put, a round is a window of time in which coaching cycles are offered. Keeping the schedule coordinated in this way, with all of the cycles starting and ending at roughly the same time, has several benefits. For example, the rounds can be tied to curriculum so that coaching cycles are aligned to units of study, there is a level of predictability and rhythm to the coach's schedule, and teachers can plan for when it might be a good time for them to engage in a coaching cycle. A school we've worked with in Colorado has built a schedule that allows for four rounds of coaching cycles. In this way, they accommodate for the ebbs and flows of the school year.

Round 1: Late September to early November

Round 2: Mid-November to winter break

Round 3: January to late February

Round 4: Mid-March to late April

What do we notice about this schedule? First, cycles do not start the first day of school. No matter how eager the teacher, everyone needs some time at the beginning of the year to get to know their students and establish classroom culture and norms. So the first round starts about three to four weeks into the year. Next, rounds do not have hard beginning and end dates. This allows for a week or so on the front end to get to know the new group of teachers; spend time in their classrooms; and create goals, learning targets, and pre-assessments. It also allows for us to have time on the back end to wrap up cycles using the Results-Based Coaching Tool (RBCT) to drive our end-of-cycle reflections. If a cycle finishes up a few days earlier or later than expected, we can accommodate for this with the flexible schedule. Lastly, you will see that there is a gap of a few weeks between Rounds 3 and 4, which would be when this school has state assessments. It is better to recognize and plan for this up front instead of being frustrated that no meaningful coaching work is happening during that time. The example that was just given has four rounds across the school year. Some coaches find this to work well, while others feel that they can manage five rounds. Taking into account the pacing of curriculum, state assessments, and the overall flow of the school calendar will help determine the number of coaching cycle rounds that will work best at a given school.

Once a schedule of rounds is determined, we can start thinking about how many coaching cycles can fit into a given round. This will vary based on the number of other duties the coach is assigned as well as on whether they are exclusively at one school or not (more on that shortly). Generally speaking, we suggest that a coach has no more than four cycles going during a given round. This allows for plenty of time for co-planning and co-teaching along with all of the other things that are part of a coach's job. If all of the cycles are with groups, then there might be room for only two or three cycles, but if there's a balance of individuals and groups, then four cycles in a round will likely be doable.

Scheduling Rounds in Multiple Schools

For those coaches who are shared between schools or who work across several schools with a specific focus (district technology coach or early childhood coach, for example), it can feel challenging to think about how to schedule rounds. Over the years, we've seen coaches do this in a number of ways that they have found to be successful. When sharing two schools, the easiest option is to divide time equally and try to get in two cycles at each school. When the schools are far apart and too much time is being wasted in travel, some coaches prefer to alternate rounds between schools. The only downside here is that it could feel disjointed to be away from the other school for up to six weeks at a time. To combat this, we recommend spending four days a week at the main school and the fifth day at the other school engaging in more informal coaching. This way relationships at the "off" school are maintained, and some openings for upcoming coaching cycles may arise from the informal work as well. Figure 6.2 illustrates the two scheduling options.

FIGURE 6.2 Options for Scheduling When Sharing Schools

Option #1—Yearlong Schedule

SCHOOL A	SCHOOL B
2.5 days per week	2.5 days per week
2 cycles per round	2 cycles per round

Option #2—Rotate Schools After Each Round

SCHOOL A	SCHOOL B
4 days per week	1 day per week
3–4 cycles	Informal coaching

For coaches who are more itinerant and are expected to be continually rotating through a number of schools, scheduling coaching in rounds can become quite complicated. In these cases, we find that if a coach can engage in one or two cycles at a time, it gives them a chance to go deep and partner with a few teachers over the course of the school year while still maintaining contact with all of the assigned schools on a regular basis. Another option is mini cycles, which were discussed in Chapter 2. If schools have site-based coaches, it's also possible for a district-level coach to partner where applicable in coaching cycles that are already happening at the school. Lastly, using a digital platform to meet virtually can be helpful when travel time becomes an issue.

Informal Coaching Still Matters

Even though we know that the biggest impact on student and teacher learning happens through the deep and ongoing work of coaching cycles, that is not to say there's no place for informal coaching. In fact, it is actually an important part of what makes Student-Centered Coaching possible. Given the fact that during a particular coaching round we can only be working with about four to eight teachers at once, we need to make sure that we aren't cutting off or ignoring the rest of the staff. Whether it's helping a teacher to find resources for an upcoming social studies unit or to get started with a new technology tool, this informal support helps us to build and strengthen relationships with teachers and to look for openings for what may be future coaching cycles. The caveat here is to be sure that the majority of our time is still spent in cycles. To be mindful of this, we suggest scheduling a few specific times each week for informal support or "office hours" when people know they can pop in and chat with you about a particular issue or need (as you may recall from the schedule from Figure 2.2 in Chapter 2).

Start Small and Gain Momentum

Oftentimes when we meet with a team of coaches in the fall of their first year with Student-Centered Coaching, at least one person will say something like "There are a few teachers on our staff who are just really reluctant, and I don't know how to get them on board." Our reply is typically "Don't worry about it!" While this may seem strange, the fact is that change takes time, and we shouldn't expect every single teacher at a school to be gung ho on day one. Instead of starting off by worrying about who *doesn't* want to work with a coach, we suggest that the focus be on those teachers who *do*. Think of these teachers as your "low-hanging fruit," and work to get a few of them engaged early on. This doesn't mean letting go of the expectation that coaching is for everyone; it just gives coaches a chance to get up and running quickly and to experience some early successes.

Another issue we encounter is that coaches are having a hard time moving out of the drive-by role and into cycles. In this case, it may work well to find someone in their school with whom they already have a good relationship and invite them to do a coaching cycle. This accomplishes several things. First, it gives the coach a presumably safe place to practice and experience success. Second, it gets a cycle going so that people can see an example of what it actually looks like. It also shows that the coach is a learner and not an expert on everything, and it hopefully creates a happy customer who will spread the word to other teachers in the building.

No matter how you get started, it's important to have realistic expectations and realize that none of this, especially if done well, will happen overnight. It's much better to start small and set yourself up for success than to book a full schedule right out of the gate and then not be able to meet people's needs. We know from research on what motivates people at work that even small wins can increase engagement in the work (Amabile & Kramer, 2011), so look for those early on and use them to gain momentum moving forward.

As we think about setting ourselves up for success, it's also important to think about the role of choice in the process. We believe "it's paramount for students to have choice, but we'd argue that it is equally important for adult learners because choice is about providing teachers with autonomy over their work. This is the beginning to authentic engagement" (Sweeney & Mausbach, 2018, p. 72). Figure 6.3 demonstrates how this can be offered through the coaching process. Building choice and ownership into coaching helps to create a true desire to partner with a coach versus participating out of a sense of compliance.

FIGURE 6.3 Providing Choice, Ownership, and Autonomy to Teachers

WHERE CHOICE CAN BE PROVIDED	HOW CHOICE CAN BE PROVIDED
Task	Teachers set their own goals for coaching cycles. Goals focus on student learning and begin with "Students will . . ." Putting the goal-setting process under the control of teachers sends the message "I am here to help you reach your goals for student learning."
Time	Teachers choose when they will participate in a coaching cycle. Using a scheduling structure with a variety of entry points provides teachers with ownership regarding when they would like to engage.
Technique	Teachers choose the instructional practices that they will integrate into their coaching cycle. This provides the opportunity to implement instruction that aligns with both the students' needs as well as the school and district expectations.
Team	Teachers choose with whom they will collaborate during coaching cycles. This breaks up existing structures such as PLCs, departments, and grade-level teams and provides fresh and purpose-driven groupings.

Source: Reprinted with permission from Sweeney & Mausbach (2018).

Be Thoughtful About Your Coaching Roster

As we saw with Katie in Chapter 5, another thing to be mindful of when trying to build momentum is to consider your coaching roster. Who you work with speaks volumes about what you believe coaching to be all about. Though it may be tempting to set an expectation that all of the new teachers will be the first ones to work with a coach—and it would easily get you started in cycles right away—what message does this give? Or if you are only working with the teachers whose students have the lowest test scores, what does this say about who coaching is for? If you want to create a culture on the belief that "we are all learners" and "coaching is about being the best we can be and not about fixing teachers," then this needs to be reflected in your roster. To show that coaching is indeed for everyone, make sure you have a balance of new and veteran teachers spanning a variety of content areas. Getting that rock star teacher into a coaching cycle early on can be one of the best things you can do to create an early success that will generate a lot of momentum moving forward.

Consistently Monitor for Impact

Back when our coaching was more teacher-centered, our work was based on the belief that "if we can just get teachers to do this (strategy, curriculum, structure), then student achievement will improve." But we came to realize that this approach is like coaching on a wing and a prayer; *hopefully* student learning will increase, but we have no way of knowing for sure. For this reason, we use the RBCT, as we learned in Chapter 3. We also need to informally monitor for impact in all aspects of our coaching work. Two of the ways we do this are through time audits and staff surveys.

Take a Close Look at How You're Spending Your Time

On Leanna's street growing up, there was a gentleman who walked from the bus stop on his way home from work every day bouncing a basketball. To all the kids in the neighborhood, he was affectionately known as "the Basketball Man." He had a job and a family and probably lots of other interests, but to them he was just the guy who dribbled a basketball all the time because that's all they ever saw him doing. This same thing can happen as coaches. If most of your time is spent managing and monitoring state tests, people will think you are "the assessment person." If the majority of your work is in running PLCs, then you will be the "PLC facilitator." If you want to be seen as the *instructional coach*, then it stands to reason that the majority of your time should be spent in coaching cycles. While there is no exact science to this number, we generally suggest that coaches shoot for spending at least 60 percent of their coaching time in cycles. This takes into account that there will be a standing meeting with the principal and perhaps with other coaches in the district, professional development, and informal coaching built into a coach's schedule as well. These things are certainly important, but if a coach isn't spending more than half of his or her time in cycles, it would be hard to imagine that this will be seen as what their job is supposed to be, making it harder to have the impact on student learning that we would hope for.

Regular calendar reviews can provide powerful insights into how our time is actually being spent. Coding weekly schedules and then using a digital tool to report our time usage helps us to honestly assess where we are relative to that 60 percent. This kind of review can be done monthly, quarterly, or twice a year. Many coaches examine the data with their principal or with their coaching team, and together they can talk about trends, things that are getting in the way, and goals moving forward. Figure 6.4 offers a tool that can be used to look at time spent within coaching cycles and time spent on duties outside of coaching cycles. Here are some possible categories to consider when tracking how your time is spent:

Within coaching cycles:

- Goal setting and creating learning targets
- Creating and analyzing pre- and post-assessments
- Co-planning
- Co-teaching

Outside of coaching cycles:

- PLCs
- Standing meetings at the school or district level
- Personal planning time
- Informal coaching
- Other duties (teaching, recess, intervention, etc.)

A second way we can audit our time is by looking at who we are working with. Earlier in this chapter we discussed how it's okay to start with the early adopters and not worry about resistant teachers. But

FIGURE 6.4   Tracking Time Within and Outside of Coaching Cycles

TIME WITHIN COACHING CYCLES

COACHING CYCLE WORK ON THE COACH'S SCHEDULE	TIME ALLOCATED
Co-planning with third-grade team	40 minutes per week
Total:	

TIME OUTSIDE OF COACHING CYCLES

OTHER WORK ON THE COACH'S SCHEDULE	TIME ALLOCATED
Leading PLCs	3 hours per week
Total:	

online resources   Available for download at **resources.corwin.com/EssentialGuideforSCCoaching**

in order to have the biggest impact possible we know we ultimately need to expand our reach. One way we can monitor this is through a Status of the Faculty. This involves keeping a list or chart of all the teachers on staff, and tracking all of the different ways in which we interact with them from relationship building to a full coaching cycle. Figure 6.5 gives a partial example of the levels of interaction that a coach has with his high school staff across an entire semester.

FIGURE 6.5   Status of the Faculty

COACH: ERIC TAYLOR		DATES: AUGUST 19–DECEMBER 17			
TEACHER	RELATIONSHIP BUILDING	DELIVERING PD; LARGE OR SMALL GROUP	PROVIDING RESOURCES	INFORMAL COACHING (E.G., UNIT PLANNING)	COACHING CYCLE
Armisen, Keith (Social Studies)	X	X	X	X	X
Calloway, Sheree (Choir)		X			
Chaney, Melissa (English)	X	X	X		
Guzdar, Dinsh (Social Studies)	X	X	X	X	X
Kreutzer, Rachel (Math)	X	X	X		
Lewis, Veronica (Math)	X	X	X		
Lyons, Marie (Chemistry)		X			

Looking at this abbreviated chart, we can learn a lot about how Eric is spending his time. It's great that he has interfaced with every single person in some way through the professional development he offers on monthly early-release days. He has also worked to build relationships in a variety of different ways with most of the teachers. But so far he has only gotten into deeper coaching work with Keith and Dinsh, the two social studies teachers he had been on a team with in the past. While there is a lot to commend Eric for, we can also see where he can continue to strive to get some of the other teachers to engage in deeper and more Student-Centered Coaching work. Keeping track through a time audit such as this can provide coaches and administrators with meaningful data to assess their impact and to set goals for future work.

Get Input From Colleagues

Auditing our time through the two methods previously discussed provides valuable information about our impact as coaches. Another invaluable source of data are staff surveys. Soliciting feedback in this way allows us to hear from a broad array of voices (in addition to those in cycles, who get the exit interview) and can tell us not just about the impact teachers feel our work is having but also about the perceptions they have of the coach and the purpose of the coaching program.

It was a year and a half into Alex's tenure as an instructional coach when she and Nicole, her principal, decided to survey the staff to get feedback on the coaching initiative. Participants remained anonymous, but the survey was structured to give specific questions to people based upon the extent to which they had engaged with the coach. They asked the following questions:

- To what extent have you engaged with the coach this year?
  - Coaching cycle
  - Lesson planning
  - Receiving resources
  - Professional development

- How do you feel working with the coach has positively impacted your teaching practice?

- How has working with the coach positively impacted student learning in your classroom?

- What impact, if any, has coaching had on our school culture?

- What words would you use to describe the role of the coach?

Items were rated on a scale of one to five in each of the impact categories, and there were descriptors to choose from in identifying the coach's role. For the teachers who had worked with Alex in coaching cycles, the feedback was incredibly positive, and this gave her and Nicole a renewed burst of energy to keep prioritizing this part of the work. The item that proved to be most insightful, however, was the question about the role of the coach.

When Alex first started as an instructional coach the year before, she and Nicole worked hard to market the new position to the staff in order to help them understand what Student-Centered Coaching is and how it is different from what they may have experienced with coaching in the past. Alex was even more explicit about this at the beginning of each coaching cycle when she set norms with teachers. Yet what they found on the survey was that the majority of the staff who hadn't engaged in coaching cycles up to that point had a very different perception of Alex's role than what she and Nicole had intended. They chose descriptors such as *evaluator, administrator*, and *accountability* when identifying what they believed to be the role of the coach. With so many teachers believing Alex's role to be evaluative, no wonder they didn't want to engage with her. This feedback from the survey was disappointing to Nicole and Alex, but they realized it gave them a clear path for next steps. It would involve revisiting and relaunching their marketing campaign around Student-Centered Coaching to make sure that everyone on the staff understood it to be about partnership and collaboration toward student learning rather than about evaluating and holding teachers accountable for implementing certain strategies.

Alex and Nicole's story provides a strong case for the power of using staff surveys, in addition to time audits, to continually monitor the impact of our coaching work.

Lesson From the Field

Heather recently hosted a few fellow coaches at her K–12 school in a small town in Iowa. They were there for a coaching lab—a half-day professional learning opportunity in which a group of coaches come together for a structured observation of one of their peers. The group engaged in a thoughtful process of observing Heather co-plan and co-teach as a part of one of her coaching cycles, and then they debriefed the process together with the help of a facilitator. With time for open discussion at the end, several of the visiting coaches expressed their amazement with how well the coaching program was running at Heather's school. Eager to learn the "magic recipe," they asked if Heather could tell them about the journey she and her principal had taken to get them to this point.

Heather started by sharing that when they were first launching the coaching program, she and Krista, the principal, spent a lot of time carefully messaging the initiative to teachers so they would have a good understanding of what Student-Centered Coaching really is. They also felt it would be important for all of the teachers to have some exposure to coaching at some point during the first year. So at the beginning of the year, Krista shared to the staff that everyone was going to get the opportunity to experience coaching by signing up for a three- or four-week coaching cycle with Heather. Krista was very careful to present this as a "get to" instead of a "have to," but a schedule breaking the year into rounds with enough slots for each teacher was passed around during the meeting, making clear that she expected everyone to take advantage of the opportunity. The mentor teachers at the school were asked to take the lead by signing up first. This created a strong example around the belief about who works with a coach and set Heather up for some early successes in working with teachers who already see themselves as ongoing learners. Fitting all 36 teachers in that first year kept Heather plenty busy, but both she and Krista felt it was important to give each teacher the exposure and to create a culture that coaching is for everyone. In the coming year, cycles were extended to the full four to six weeks, and with so many teachers signing up, Krista decided to bring on another half-time coach into the program.

Another step that they took to continue the momentum with the coaching program was with what they call Synergy Sessions, which happened during the first five to ten minutes of their weekly early release days. Each of the teachers who were currently working in a coaching cycle would take a minute or two to share with the staff what they are working on relative to the goal for student learning, either through examples of student work or speaking about a strategy or resource they used to help students meet the goal. This not only highlighted the coaching work but it also underscored the notion that coaching is about partnering to serve students rather than fixing teachers. They also emphasized this message through the many ways they celebrated coaching throughout the year. This included highlighting coaching work in a monthly newsletter and having a fun celebration at the end of each coaching round. While the focus was always on student learning, they invited teachers who were interested to share about their own growth as well.

After listening to Heather, it was clear to the rest of the group that Student-Centered Coaching is embedded into every aspect of teaching and learning at her school. Krista made it clear that she expected everyone to engage in coaching cycles and she gave Heather the time necessary to do it. Additionally, they constantly highlighted the work that was being done and reinforced the notion that coaching is about continuing to learn and grow as professionals in order to best serve all students.

Tools and Techniques

Understanding the value of coaching cycles is an important first step, but making them an expected and regular part of the way coaching happens takes some work. See Figure 6.6 for the Checklist for Getting Coaching Cycles Up and Running. We recommend using this tool when first getting going with Student-Centered Coaching, and it can also be useful as a self-assessment from time to time to make sure that you are staying on track with the commitment to coaching in this way.

FIGURE 6.6   Checklist for Getting Coaching Cycles Up and Running

Calibrate With the Principal:

❑ Principal allocates time for the coach to partner with teachers. *Be specific about what coaches will (and will not) be doing with their time.*

❑ Principal and coach define the coach's role. *What's the purpose for coaching? Why is it important? What will the coach do?*

❑ Principal and coach describe how coaching aligns with other district initiatives. *Make sure that teachers understand that coaching isn't "one more thing."*

❑ Principal describes the expectations for teacher participation. *Who participates? What does participation look like? How much time will it take?*

❑ Principal describes how teachers will be provided with choice and ownership. *How is coaching about more than compliance? Where is there choice for teachers?*

❑ Principal and coach define their roles. *Where is there overlap? What is distinct?*

❑ Principal and coach meet on a weekly basis. *How are the coaching cycles going? How can we align them with other PD opportunities?*

Launch Cycles:

❑ Coach captures openings from teachers (survey, letter, etc.) for the first round of coaching cycles. *Who is ready to go?*

❑ Coach creates a schedule for the first round of coaching cycles. *How will the coach spend his or her time for the next four to six weeks? Schedule the first round of coaching cycles on paper, and share it with teachers.*

❑ Coach visits the classrooms of teachers who are in the first round of coaching cycles. *Coach gets to know the teacher and students before coaching begins.*

During Cycles:

❑ Coach has a goal-setting conversation with the teachers who are in the first round of coaching cycles. *What are the teachers' goals for student learning? How will we pre-assess students?*

❑ Coach and teacher set agreements for how they will work together. *How will we co-plan and co-teach?*

❑ Coach ends the first round of cycles with an exit interview. *How did it go? What can I do differently next time?*

❑ Principal and coach determine how they will celebrate the impact of the first round of coaching cycles. *How did the students and teachers grow? How can we use the Results-Based Coaching Tool (RBCT)?*

❑ Coach repeats the process for scheduling the next round of coaching cycles. *How will we engage different teachers? How can the principal provide support and encouragement?*

As we work to implement a Student-Centered Coaching model, it's important to keep in mind the systems we need to put into place to support the work. We may encounter roadblocks along the way, so here are some strategies to keep the work moving forward (see Figure 6.7). The if/then charts at the end of each chapter can also be found in Resource A in this book.

FIGURE 6.7 Strategies for Making Coaching Cycles Happen

IF I HEAR OR NOTICE . . .	THEN I CAN SAY OR DO . . .
"This is a new position for me, and I want to be seen as being useful to teachers, so I'm really willing to do whatever they ask of me."	Remember that a coach will be defined by how people see them spending their time. Therefore, it's important to get started with coaching cycles. Maybe there's a teacher or two who they can invite to participate in a cycle to practice and get some momentum.

(Continued)

FIGURE 6.7 (Continued)

IF I HEAR OR NOTICE . . .	THEN I CAN SAY OR DO . . .
"We just completed a time audit at the end of the first semester, and I'm barely getting into coaching cycles because there are so many other things taking up my time."	This is great data to share with the principal and building leadership team. Together, they can think creatively about ways to clear the coaches' plate to make more time to engage in cycles.
"It's the end of the first year with Student-Centered Coaching, and I worked with the same handful of teachers all year long. I couldn't seem to get others to engage."	This is a good time to reflect on the marketing that's been done throughout the year. How can you continue to help people understand what Student-Centered Coaching is and why it matters, especially the teachers who have yet to engage in coaching cycles?

A Final Thought

There's a saying that "anything worth doing is worth doing well." This holds true for running a sports camp in the neighborhood as much as it does for coaching. Simply bringing a coach on board does not ensure that coaching will take root at a school—particularly not in a way that is centered around outcomes for student learning. For Student-Centered Coaching to thrive, it takes thoughtful implementation of a number of systems and structures. Without these, a coach can get stuck in the land of drive-by coaching, providing resources, and doing countless other jobs in the school that don't have much to do with being a coach. This results in a valuable position at the school having little to no impact on student learning and possibly to negative feelings toward coaching on the part of teachers.

When coaches and principals take the time to "do it well," then Student-Centered Coaching becomes a vital and integral part of both teacher and student learning.

Supporting and Evaluating Coaches

7

On a sunny spring morning, Leanna greeted a room of about seventy instructional coaches. Many of them had been coaching for several years, and she had been brought in to guide the implementation of Student-Centered Coaching in their district. This would be her last day with them, and she wanted to set a tone for reflection as well as celebrate the learning they had done together over the past two years.

In honor of Teacher Appreciation Day, which had taken place a few days prior, SoulPancake and Edutopia (2014) published a video titled *If I Knew Then: A Letter to Me on My First Day Teaching*. Leanna shared this touching video in which several teachers write and then read aloud the advice they would give to themselves if they could go back to their first day on the job. She then asked the group what advice they would give to themselves on their first day as new coaches.

The room was silent as they busily penned their letters. Then they stood in small groups and shared with each other. Leanna listened as several coaches read their letters aloud. Here's some of what she heard:

- *Halfway through the year, you still won't feel like you know what you're doing, but give yourself time and grace.*

- *Never give up, and always greet each day with enthusiasm.*

- *You're going to miss the classroom, but remember that you're still making an impact on kids.*

- *Coaching is very different from teaching. Know that ahead of time.*

- *Not everyone will appreciate what you do or understand what your role is, but don't give up.*

- *There will be rough days and weeks, but use all of this to keep learning.*

- *Breathe slowly and cry when you need to.*

- *Don't forget to smile and laugh!*

It was clear that everyone understood how dramatic the shift is from teaching to coaching, and everyone knew that support and encouragement are essential to a coach's success.

We also remember moving into a coaching role ourselves. Not only did we miss the connections we had with our students but we were also coaching in schools without a clearly articulated model. Even though the coaches in Leanna's group weren't expected to figure it out on their own, their letters underscored the fact that it takes a lot of support to coach in a way that impacts student and teacher learning.

In this chapter we will introduce a variety of methods for supporting to coaches. This includes hiring the right people, implementing job-embedded professional learning structures, developing a curriculum of support, and using tools to evaluate coaches that align with the practices for Student-Centered Coaching. It's not enough to simply offer words of encouragement to coaches, telling them that "everything will be okay." Most will need more than that. The tools and strategies in this chapter are designed to provide them with the support they deserve.

First Things First: Hire Effective Coaches

It's exciting when districts find the resources to hire coaches. When creating a plan for hiring , it's imperative for districts to get clear on the philosophy and practices for coaching first and then staffing the positions later.

It all begins with the job description. Recently, we reviewed a job description that was created by a district that was implementing Student-Centered Coaching. We noticed that the duties listed prioritized practices such as (1) modeling lessons, (2) writing curriculum, and (3) managing Tier 2 interventions. We pointed out that these practices aren't emphasized in Student-Centered Coaching and suggested that it might be confusing to include them so prominently. Imagine getting hired as a coach with the understanding that you'll be managing Tier 2 interventions and then learning that the real expectation is to engage in coaching cycles. Luckily, we caught the lack of alignment early and worked with the district to revise the job description to feature the core practices for Student-Centered Coaching. This gave the candidates clarity regarding what the role of coach would entail. Figure 7.1 is what we created.

FIGURE 7.1   Student-Centered Coaching Job Description

Description: The instructional coach will use the practices for Student-Centered Coaching to provide support to teachers across grade levels and subjects. Coaching will be driven by student outcomes and will lead to the implementation of effective instructional practices in the classroom.

Coaching Practice

- Have experience with, or a willingness to learn, how to implement the core practices for Student-Centered Coaching.
- Facilitate Student-Centered Coaching cycles across grade levels and disciplines.
- Use student evidence when co-planning lessons with teachers.
- Use the co-teaching moves for Student-Centered Coaching when working in classrooms.
- Collaborate with teachers to design and use formative assessments.
- Create opportunities for discourse among teachers and students.
- Work with teachers to ensure student ownership, engagement, and choice.
- Provide informal support to teachers in the areas of classroom management, curriculum design, or other expressed needs.
- Collaborate with teachers to create a culture of rigor, inquiry, and reflection by probing ideas and further pressing students to explore their intellect.
- Engage in weekly meetings with the principal to discuss the implementation of Student-Centered Coaching.

Collaborative Practice or Learning Stance

- Partner with the principal to build a culture for coaching.
- Build trusting, respectful, and professional relationships with teachers.
- Engage in reflective dialogue with others.
- Model being a reflective practitioner and support others to reflect as well.
- Maintain a friendly, flexible, and collaborative disposition.

(Continued)

FIGURE 7.1 (Continued)

Curriculum and Professional Learning

- Collaborate with colleagues to facilitate professional learning.
- Work with teams of teachers to unpack curricular units.
- Assist with the development of district curriculum, instruction, and assessments.
- Demonstrate presentation skills for conducting professional learning.

What to Look For When Hiring Coaches

Finding a coach with all of the right qualities can sometimes feel like you are looking for a unicorn. That's because being an effective coach requires a special combination of knowledge, skills, and a learning-focused disposition. When hiring coaches, we suggest focusing on two areas: (1) knowledge of pedagogy and (2) a disposition of curiosity and openness.

You may have noticed that experience with coaching isn't on the list. Nor is content expertise. This is because being an effective coach isn't predicated on coaching experience or content knowledge. Rather, it's about supporting teachers to plan, reflect, and adjust in ways that promote student learning. We've found that with support, coaches can learn how to implement the practices for Student-Centered Coaching, while disposition and interpersonal skills are much harder to teach.

Knowledge of Pedagogy

Knowledge of pedagogy means coaches have a track record of implementing effective instruction. But that's not enough. They must also understand how to support teachers to implement high-quality instruction themselves. Without this, coaches will lack credibility and may not support teachers to make decisions that will increase student learning.

Zeroing in on the pedagogical practices that we expect for coaches to carry into their role helps districts select coaches who will hit the ground running. Figure 7.2 provides examples of instructional practices that readily transfer across subjects and grade levels. These are what we seek out during the hiring process.

FIGURE 7.2 Examples of Transferable Pedagogy

- Crafting student friendly learning targets
- Using formative assessments that make learning visible
- Planning lessons that are learning, rather than activity, focused
- Building student self-assessment and reflection into lessons
- Designing methods for increasing student discourse
- Differentiating lessons, such as through conferring and small-group instruction
- Using student evidence to plan lessons
- Using effective strategies for classroom management

A Disposition of Curiosity and Openness

Wondering is more powerful than knowing, especially since classrooms are such complex places. We can't underestimate how far being a learner can take a coach. Hiring for soft skills like curiosity and openness contributes to creating a culture that is learning focused and maintains a growth mindset. In Chapter 4 we discussed the importance of asking before telling. This simply can't happen when coaches think they have all of the answers. Entering into conversations with an open mind and an interest in learning alongside the teacher is how we encourage teachers to take a learning stance.

It can be scary to operate in a space of curiosity. That's because it requires confidence and the belief that great ideas can be built together. We both found this to be challenging when we were novice coaches because we thought we should carry all of the ideas and then share them with others. The result was that we carried the learning too, meaning we did the thinking instead of creating the space for teachers to do so. This isn't how we build capacity in others.

Seeking out people with a learning disposition is an important part of the hiring process. One way we can achieve this is by sharing complex scenarios during the interview process and then asking what steps they would take in this situation. We would hope to hear that candidates would seek to understand *first* and then share strategies *second*. This puts the coach squarely in the category of learner. Conversely, we would be concerned if the candidate shared all of the things they would *do* to solve the problem, as this isn't a learning stance.

Another way we learn the disposition of coaching candidates is to ask them to describe a situation when they were a learner. Here we'd hope to tap into not only how the person navigated new learning but what their mindset was throughout the process. Understanding the candidate's mindset provides insight regarding how comfortable they are navigating the unknown.

How Curiosity and Openness Merge With Pedagogical Understanding

Diane had been teaching fourth and fifth grade before she transitioned to become a literacy coach. Pretty quickly, the realization set in that she would be coaching in grade levels that she had never taught. When envisioning what this would look like, she knew that carrying herself as an expert wouldn't be authentic. She also knew that credibility was important. She had to find a way to bridge that gap.

Her first step was to approach Lori, a skilled and respected kindergarten teacher. Diane explained that she wanted to learn about teaching emergent readers and writers and wondered if she could spend some time in Lori's classroom. As a very busy kindergarten teacher, Lori was thrilled to have an extra set of hands and Diane began working with her a few afternoons each week.

Pretty soon, Lori asked if they could plan lessons together. She valued Diane's perspective and wanted to run some ideas by her. Over time, their work shifted to look more like a coaching cycle. During these conversations, Lori brought most of the content, and Diane was able to think with her about how the students might engage, be grouped, and be assessed. While she was glad that her knowledge of pedagogy turned out to add value to their planning sessions, she still had to do her homework. This included studying the stages and characteristics of emergent readers, taking advantage of relevant professional development opportunities, and working to apply what she knew about second-language acquisition to a kindergarten context. Diane had been worried that she had to be an "expert" and was more than a little bit relieved to realize that being a learner was what really mattered.

This experience is often even more pronounced in secondary schools where coaches may work across a vast array of subjects and content areas. As with Lori, the key is for coaches to understand pedagogy and then figure out how it transfers to the context where they will be coaching. All of this rests on a foundation of curiosity and openness.

Provide Job-Embedded Support Through Coaching Labs

We know that teachers need job-embedded opportunities for professional learning. But let's not forget that coaches do too. While it can be valuable for coaches to attend conferences, read professional texts, and meet with district leaders, nothing takes us further than providing support that is rooted in our own school communities. We accomplish this through coaching labs.

Coaching labs take us deeper into the practices and decision-making of effective coaching. They are not exemplars of coaching but rather are examples of authentic coaching that stretch our thinking. The process involves a prebrief that provides time for the coach to set the focus and share tools and strategies that have been used. Then an observation of coaching is followed by a debrief to unpack implications and points of learning.

Any coach is a good candidate to host a coaching lab because the philosophy is one of peer learning rather than being an expert. If a district has hired coaches with the stance of learner, then there shouldn't be any problem recruiting a coaching lab host. When planning coaching labs, we take the following considerations into account:

- Coaching lab hosts aren't experts; they are learners. We are observing to expand our thinking, generate questions, and develop a view of what Student-Centered Coaching looks like in our schools.

- Coaching labs occur over a half day and include between eight to ten observers.

- Coaching labs are authentic examples of our work. They are not about showcasing practice.

- Coaching labs adhere to a protocol and norms for the observation.

Coaching labs are led by a facilitator who provides support before, during, and after the observation. It is essential for the facilitator to use a protocol as it keeps the conversation objective and learning focused. We have adjusted the protocol for coaching labs over the years, and Figure 7.3 provides our most current thinking.

FIGURE 7.3   Student-Centered Coaching Lab Protocol

Goal for the Coaching Cycle:

Learning Target(s) for the Lesson:

Prebrief (30–45 minutes)	The facilitator introduces the protocol and shares the norms for the observation. The coach provides background about the coaching work that is taking place with the teacher or team of teachers. This includes sharing the learning target(s) and plan for the lesson. The coach may also choose to share tools, logs, and artifacts that have been used to organize the coaching work. Participants are invited to ask clarifying questions. **Observation Norms for Coaching Labs** • Come with a positive attitude, and be a learner. We are not here to critique or give feedback to the coach or teacher. • Avoid side conversations. Please do not speak to students unless it has been an established part of the process. • Get close to the action by collecting student evidence during the lesson. A note catcher will be provided for this purpose. • Be ready to think through the entire process. This includes the prebrief, observation, and debrief. Participants are expected to be a part of the full process, rather than popping into certain portions. Note: The teacher does not attend the prebrief.
Observe the Co-Teaching Session (30–45 minutes)	Participants observe the teacher and coach as they work together in the classroom. Observers practice noticing and naming during this part of the process. The facilitator provides a note catcher (see Figure 7.4) for this purpose.

Observe the Co-Planning Session (30–45 minutes)	Participants observe as the teacher and coach co-plan using the student evidence that was gathered during the lesson. While observing, participants take notes to capture the coaching moves and language that are used.
Debrief the Coaching (60 minutes)	Participants debrief in the following rounds. During the first three rounds, the lab host is a silent observer. Then the host joins in after Round 3 to answer questions and share thinking. **Round 1: What happened?** • Participants take turns describing what they noticed during either part of the observation. The focus may be on the student learning, coaching moves, coaching language, etc. Use objective language, such as "I saw," "I heard," "I noticed." **Round 2: What does it mean?** • Participants share implications for student and teacher learning that surfaced as a result of the observation. A possible stem is "Because . . . then . . ." **Round 3: What do I wonder?** • Participants share questions that were elicited as a result of the observation. These can be about either the observation itself or something related to their own coaching practice. The facilitator collects the questions that are then addressed by the coach. **Round 4: What are my next steps?** • Participants share a next step for their own learning. Note: The teacher does not attend the debrief.

online resources 🔖 Available for download at **resources.corwin.com/EssentialGuideforSCCoaching**

Collecting Student Evidence During Coaching Labs

Coaching labs are the perfect opportunity to practice collecting student evidence using the strategy of noticing and naming. In *Student-Centered Coaching: The Moves*, we define noticing and naming as a "dynamic process that takes place when a teacher and coach work side by side in the classroom to surface what the students are doing well and where they have potential to grow" (Sweeney & Harris, 2017, p. 60).

We achieve this by providing each participant with a student evidence note catcher (see Figure 7.4). This tool guides the observers away from talking with (or teaching) the students, or only focusing on the instruction. Instead, they use the learning targets that were identified during the prebrief to practice formatively assessing throughout the lesson, which is one of our most important coaching moves. Students may not be used to a group of adults listening intently to their learning, but we've found most don't mind showing what they know, and they usually go on about their business.

A few minutes before the lesson ends, we ask the coaching lab participants to do a quick analysis of their notes in order to identify a few patterns or trends that they noticed. Participants are then able to anticipate the discussion that will follow between the teacher and hosting coach during the planning conversation. This reminds us that coaching is about understanding where students are right now and then working together to decide where to go next.

Who Facilitates Coaching Labs?

Coaching labs are most often facilitated by a district leader or, in our case, a consultant from our team. The facilitator is responsible for the planning and facilitation of the lab itself. This includes setting and maintaining norms, keeping the conversation learning focused, and making sure the coach and teacher are comfortable throughout the process. The following qualities are what we look for in a coaching lab facilitator:

- Has experience using protocols to lead productive and nonjudgmental conversations.

- Is able to make connections from what was observed to the core practices for Student-Centered Coaching.

- Listens and probes for specificity throughout the process.

- Ensures that all voices are heard.

- Understands how to keep the group focused on coaching and not get distracted by programs or instruction.

- Sets norms for the observation and intervenes when norms aren't kept.

FIGURE 7.4   Note Catcher for Coaching Labs

Goal for the Coaching Cycle:

Learning Target(s) for the Lesson:

Collection of Student Evidence Using the Learning Targets

Name:	Name:	Name:
Name:	Name:	Name:
Name:	Name:	Name:
Name:	Name:	**TRENDS:**

What Happened?

"I saw, I heard, I noticed . . . "

What Does It Mean?

"Because . . . then . . . "

What Do I Wonder?

"I'm wondering. . . I'd like to think more about . . . "

What Are My Next Steps?

"Now I'm going to . . . "

online resources ⇲   Available for download at **resources.corwin.com/EssentialGuideforSCCoaching**

- Keeps an eye on the time.

- Follows up afterward with the lab host to provide personalized feedback.

- Provides a joyful environment for the coaching lab (such as snacks and celebrations).

Planning for Coaching Labs

About a week before a coaching lab, the facilitator meets with the hosting coach to discuss (1) background on the coach's work; (2) which teacher, or teachers, will be included; (3) what the schedule will look like; and (4) other information that will be important for the observers to understand. The schedule is often the hardest part of the planning process. We suggest identifying the time frame for the lesson first and then going from there. Sometimes a coach requests to include only the co-planning portion of the observation or to plan first and teach the lesson second. We try to remain flexible and always encourage the lesson component because it provides context that can't be achieved by simply observing a coaching conversation. That said, we also recognize that we need to take the coach's readiness and the timing of the coaching cycle into account.

Thoughtful planning is key to ensure that the lab is well run and that the lab host feels comfortable with the process. It helps us get the most out of the coaching lab experience.

A Curriculum to Support New Coaches

Just like the seasons, new coaches typically move through a series of predictable stages in their development across the first year. In the first few weeks of school, they are full of enthusiasm. Then, as the leaves begin to fall, coaches may begin to feel discouraged as the complexity of the job becomes clearer.

Just as we have learned to predict this "October slump," we have created a curriculum for supporting coaches that matches the rhythm of the seasons. Aligning support with the stages of the school year demands for a district to anticipate and address challenges as they come. Figure 7.5 provides a year at a glance for new coaches and serves as a tool for developing a curriculum of coaching support that does just that.

FIGURE 7.5 Supporting New Coaches

	COMMON CHALLENGES FOR NEW COACHES	SUPPORT FOR NEW COACHES
Fall: August Through November	Early in the year, most new coaches are transitioning away from the classroom, and they often worry about how to most effectively spend their time. October is often the toughest month for new coaches, as they gradually become more concerned regarding how to make an impact on student learning.	At this stage, new coaches benefit from collaborative learning that is rooted in their day-to-day work. Topics include the following: • Building a partnership with the school leader • Fostering relationships with teachers • Understanding the core practices for Student-Centered Coaching • Launching coaching cycles • Building a schedule for the first few months of the school year • Using the Results-Based Coaching Tool (RBCT) to measure the impact of coaching cycles
Winter: November Through February	By now, most coaches have been in coaching cycles, likely with the most engaged teachers. They'll need to develop strategies for gaining entry with teachers who have not yet become involved. It is also important to reinforce the importance of measuring our impact. At this stage in the year, we support (and expect) coaches to use the RBCT to measure the impact of their coaching cycles.	At this stage, new coaches benefit from collaboration with colleagues, coaching labs, and one-on-one problem-solving sessions. Topics include the following: • Building relationships with teachers who haven't engaged in a coaching cycle • Launching the next round of coaching cycles to include more teachers • Continuing to refine the use of the core practices for Student-Centered Coaching • Using the RBCT to measure the impact of coaching cycles • Participating in coaching labs • Using time audits to reflect on impact throughout the school

(Continued)

FIGURE 7.5   (Continued)

	COMMON CHALLENGES FOR NEW COACHES	SUPPORT FOR NEW COACHES
Spring: March Through May	The spring testing season arrives, and this may throw off the schedule for coaching cycles. During this stage, we recommend that coaches focus on grade levels or subjects that aren't tested. Or it may be necessary to spend a few weeks supporting the testing process. Coaches may elect to engage in mini coaching cycles that last just a few weeks and focus on gaps in student performance that teachers would like to address before the end of the year.	At this stage, new coaches benefit from continued collaboration with colleagues, coaching labs, and one-on-one problem-solving sessions. Topics include the following: • Reflecting on the use of the RBCT and how coaching has impacted student learning and teacher practice • Setting goals and planning for the next year • Participating in coaching labs • Using time audits to reflect on impact throughout the school

Tools and Processes for Evaluating Coaches

How we evaluate coaches connects directly with how we support them. Much like the job description, we must align our evaluation tools to the practices for Student-Centered Coaching. We've seen plenty of districts pull out whatever teacher or specialist rubric exists and then use it with the coaches. But if our evaluation tools don't align with the day-to-day work of coaches, then the very process of evaluation will become a less than useful exercise. To serve this purpose, we created the Rubric for Student-Centered Coaching. It includes seven domains that are descriptors for effective coaching (see Figure 7.6). It also includes a success criteria for each domain. Coaches, and those who evaluate them, can use the rubric as a road map for continuous professional learning. The complete rubric can be found in Resource D of this book.

FIGURE 7.6   Domains on the Rubric for Student-Centered Coaching

1. The coach understands and implements the core practices for Student-Centered Coaching.

2. The coach designs systems and structures to engage teachers in coaching cycles.

3. The coach understands effective instruction and helps teachers implement it.

4. The coach builds trusting and respectful relationships with teachers.

5. The coach provides skilled facilitation during collaboration and professional learning.

6. The coach maintains a learning stance.

7. The coach engages in reflective dialogue with teachers.

Using the Rubric for Student-Centered Coaching

The rubric can serve as a centerpiece for both professional learning and evaluation of coaches. Some districts begin the year by asking coaches to select a domain to focus on. This then becomes their professional learning goal for the year. Others ask the coaching team to agree on one domain to practice, and then the rubric is used to guide their professional learning.

We also recommend for principals to regularly observe coaches as they engage in goal setting, developing learning targets, co-planning, co-teaching, or the reflection that occurs at the end of a coaching cycle. On these occasions, the rubric is used to provide the coach with strengths-based feedback, a process that was described in Chapter 4. Annie, an elementary principal who supports a team of coaches in her school, recently remarked that engaging in this process is time well spent because she is able to connect with students, the teacher, and the coach, all at the same time.

Another way to use the Rubric for Student-Centered Coaching is during conversations that are part of the formal evaluation process. Just like with teacher evaluation, an aligned framework is essential to ground the conversation in the practices that are expected. The rubric serves this purpose by anchoring the process in objective descriptors of effective coaching practice.

Lastly, we've found that the rubric can be used to guide principals to understand what to expect with coaching in their school. During a recent workshop, Diane led a group of principals through a calibration session in which they watched videos of coaching and discussed how they would use the rubric to evaluate the conversation and what feedback they would provide. Engaging in this work helped the principals understand the specific behaviors and practices that we are looking for as we implement Student-Centered Coaching.

The Role of the District in Supporting Student-Centered Coaching

Working with adult learners is multifaceted and demanding. Coaches need a tremendous amount of support if they are going to make the impact we are looking for. This may come from school administrators, district level leaders, or both. In the article "Pave the Way for Coaches," Heineke and Polnick (2013) write, "As administrators step up to the plate and provide support for instructional coaching, they will ensure that the money and time invested in professional learning will pay off with greater dividends in sustained teacher growth and student achievement" (p. 51). While much of this support occurs at the school level, we can't neglect the important role that the district plays as well.

Keep the Lines of Communication Open Between Coaches, Principals, and the District

Our work is adversely affected when communication breaks down among coaches, principals, and the district. This is especially true when the different parties carry their own definition of the coach's roles and responsibilities. Getting on the same page, and establishing clear lines of communication, are paramount. We recommend for district leaders to spend time shadowing coaches or attending coaching labs so that they understand the complexity of the work. This is especially important when districts are focusing on implementing a new program or initiative. Getting into schools to experience the work is one of the best ways to build bridges among the coach, principal, and district.

Establish Expectations for Coaches to Evaluate the Impact of Coaching

Throughout this book, you've been introduced to a variety of tools for evaluating the impact of coaching. The most important tool we use is the Results-Based Coaching Tool (RBCT). While a first step for school leaders is to set the expectation that coaches are engaging in coaching cycles most of the time, the next step is to ensure that they are using the tool to evaluate the impact of their coaching cycles.

When districts set forth the expectation for coaches to monitor their impact, they are providing a measure of accountability throughout the system. This protects coaches from the vulnerable position of not quantifying their impact. It also reinforces the important role they play in our schools.

Find the Time to Provide Support to Coaches

There is a push and pull when it comes to removing coaches from their schools for the purpose of professional learning. As an assistant superintendent recently put it, "We have to give the coaches the support they need, but we can't do it at the expense of the teachers and students in their schools." The struggle is real.

Most districts establish consistent meeting times for coaches. This is important so that the team is on the same page, is feeling supported, and has opportunities to problem solve barriers they are facing. We suggest for these meetings to be just a few hours each week; otherwise we may be taking coaches out of their schools too often.

It can be useful to look at the full year to find pockets of time when coaching isn't in high gear and plan more intensive professional learning to take place during these windows of time. For example, teachers aren't ready for coaching cycles in the first few weeks of school, so this is the perfect time for coaches to engage in collaborative learning. Other opportune times may be when teachers are busy testing, are wrapping things up before breaks, or are involved in parent-teacher conferences. If we are strategic and consider the rhythm of a school's calendar, then we will find opportunities when we can provide coaches with professional learning that isn't at the expense of their coaching work in schools.

Lesson From the Field

It was Diane's first year of working with coaches in a small district that was implementing Student-Centered Coaching. She started with a two-day launch with the coaches, principals, and other district administrators in late summer. As they were wrapping up on the second day, she shared that they would be holding a coaching lab as part of her next visit. She then took some time to explain the philosophy and process for the lab and answered their questions. A useful tool for this conversation was a coaching lab overview that describes the process and how the hosting coach is supported (included in Resource E).

The district curriculum coordinator worried that they wouldn't get a coach to volunteer so early in the year and was pleasantly surprised when one of the high school coaches immediately raised her hand to say she was willing to jump in and give it a try.

The week prior to a visit in late October, Diane scheduled a planning call with Janelle, the coach who had volunteered to host the lab. After thanking Janelle for her willingness to take the lead, they jumped right into scheduling the observation. Once Diane was confident that they had enough time blocked out for the prebrief, observation, and debrief, she was ready to guide Janelle through planning the content for the lab.

Janelle shared that she was in a coaching cycle with Cody, an English language arts (ELA) teacher. They were working on the goal *Students will write an opinion piece that takes a stand on a current topic and will use a variety of relevant sources to support their position* with his ninth-grade class. At this point, the students had chosen their topic and were in the early stages of research.

There was concern that the students would simply type their topic in the search browser and choose the first thing that popped up without any critical examination. Therefore, they would be focusing on the learning target *I can assess the relevance and validity of a source as it relates to my topic.* Students would use a graphic organizer to track and analyze their sources based on a set of criteria they generated in class. Janelle thought that for the lab, the other coaches could listen in as they analyzed the student work to see how the students were progressing toward the target and plan for next steps in instruction.

Diane was impressed with how far along Janelle was this early in her coaching. She pointed out that the lab would be a rich learning opportunity for the participating coaches as well. While observations of co-planning are a great way to see coaching in action, Diane wondered if they might be able to see Janelle co-teaching as well. When asked about the possibility, Janelle demurred. "I have to admit that I haven't really done any co-teaching yet. I spent some time in Cody's room observing and getting to know the students, but I'm not really sure how to take it to the next level," she confessed. "I totally get it," Diane replied. "Co-teaching can be the most challenging part of coaching. But what if we looked at this as an opportunity? I can help you with the co-teaching part, and that will enable the other coaches to see what this aspect of coaching can look like." Janelle paused for a moment and then said, "The thought makes me nervous and excited all at once. It's a lot to think of doing something new in front of the other coaches, but I like the idea of pushing myself to try." Diane reminded her that the lab is not about perfection but about learning together from authentic coaching experiences.

With Diane's guidance, they mapped out a plan to get Janelle ready for co-teaching. First, she would ask Cody if she could use this lab experience as an opportunity to try something new as a coach. Then she would share the co-teaching moves to give Cody a sense of the kinds of things that would be happening when they were working in the classroom together. To read more about these co-teaching moves, check out *Student-Centered Coaching: The Moves* (Sweeney & Harris, 2017). During the lab observation, she would use the coaching log for co-planning (see Figure 2.5 in Chapter 2) to ensure they were explicit about who would be doing what during the lesson. Armed with next steps, they wrapped up the conversation, both sharing how much they were looking forward to the lab the following week.

The day of the lab came, and it went off without a hitch. The other coaches observed as Janelle and Cody taught and planned together. Then they shared their thinking during the debrief. Throughout the conversation, it was clear that lots of new learning had taken place. Janelle shared how glad she was to be pushed out of her comfort zone to try co-teaching. And feedback from the participating coaches revealed how much they benefited from being able to observe this key piece of coaching as well.

Tools and Techniques

With a well-crafted job description in hand, it's time to consider the processes for interviewing coaches. We find that it is important to assess not only verbal but also written communication. For this reason, we recommend using a two-part process that includes both (see Figure 7.7). Throughout the interviews, we recommend listening for three characteristics in this ranked order: (1) a learning stance that implies curiosity and openness, (2) a clear understanding of pedagogy, and (3) the confidence to get in there and coach. As we mentioned earlier, less prioritized are the candidates' experiences with coaching or specific content expertise.

There is no question that hiring a team of effective coaches takes time and attention. Not only are we gauging the candidates' experience but we are also thinking about interpersonal skills and content knowledge. Figure 7.8 provides strategies to support you as you work through these important decisions. The if/then charts at the end of each chapter can also be found in Resource A in this book.

FIGURE 7.7   Questions for Interviewing Coaches

The following screening questions are completed in writing:

1. What specific skills or attributes do you believe are necessary to be successful in this role?
2. How would you support teachers to reach their goals for student learning?
3. What primary coaching practices would you use? Why?

The following questions are asked in an interview format. Ideally school and district leaders are in attendance, as might be teacher leaders or other coaches:

1. How do you learn best?
2. What do you value about working with adult learners?
3. Why are you interested in pursuing the role of the coach?
4. If you were faced with this scenario (share a coaching scenario), what would you do?
5. How do you see yourself building relationships with teachers and the principal?
6. What pedagogical background do you have that will support you in this role?
7. How will you organize your time as a coach?
8. Would you share a professional book you've read lately? Tell us about it.

FIGURE 7.8 Language and Strategies for Hiring Effective Coaches

IF I HEAR OR NOTICE . . .	THEN I MIGHT THINK OR DO . . .
There are two candidates for a coaching position. One has worked at the school for twenty years. The other is from out of the district. Since coaching is built on relationships, it seems like a good idea to hire her. But the principal hesitates because it feels like teachers will perceive the hiring process as not being thorough or objective.	Formalizing (and de-personalizing) the hiring process is an important step. One option is to use the domains that are included on the Rubric for Student-Centered Coaching to make the expectations for the coaching role clear. It is also important to articulate that the rubric will be used for evaluation processes. This moves the hiring process away from relationships and toward the practices and dispositions that are expected.
During an interview, a candidate for a high school coaching position says, "I see myself working with the math and science departments because I'm familiar with these subjects." When the principal hears this, he isn't sure how to respond because he doesn't want to hire a coach who lacks the confidence that is required to coach across content areas.	The principal may say, "What we are looking for is an understanding of pedagogy that stretches across content. We also value coaches who carry a learning disposition. That said, we are prepared to help you develop the skills that you will need as a coach." It's important to keep in mind that anyone who steps into the job must understand that we can't pick and choose who we work with. Rather, a coach must be confident enough to work with teachers across the faculty.
Thanks to support from the school board, the district posted job descriptions for twelve new coaching positions. So far, only four people have applied. The assistant superintendent knows that this is their chance to build an effective team of coaches but wonders why nobody wants the job.	Sometimes it's important to "go slow to go fast," and this may be one of those times. Doing some research to gather perceptions by teachers about coaching would help the district understand why teachers are not interested. We'd suggest to hold off on hiring any coaches until there is both a deeper candidate pool and a better understanding of the coaching role throughout the teaching ranks.

A Final Thought

Supporting coaches (and a coaching effort) can be challenging. It demands a vision that meets the requirements of the system while also addressing the needs of the individual coach. What we can't do is simply assume that coaches are smart people who will figure it out on their own. Taking this approach puts coaches in a lonely position and can disrupt the entire coaching model.

As the coaches revealed in their letters to themselves, coaching is hard work and takes a lot of encouragement. But uplifting words of support aren't enough. When coaches are provided with the opportunity to learn together, reflect, and problem solve, we are able to create touchstone experiences that lead to their growth and development. In turn, this leads to greater outcomes throughout the system, which translates into better learning for students and for teachers.

Resource A

If/Then Charts

Language for Making a Shift to Student-Centered Coaching

IF I HEAR . . .	THEN I CAN USE THE FOLLOWING LANGUAGE . . .
"I don't see any need to do a whole coaching cycle right now. Can you just help me with a few ideas for my upcoming unit?"	"I am happy to brainstorm some ideas with you, but I believe we can have a much bigger impact if we could partner throughout the whole unit. That way we can try different things along the way and make adjustments based on how the students are responding."
"I feel pretty good with the new math program, so I don't think you need to come in and give me any help with it."	"I'm glad to hear you're feeling good about the new program. My job as a coach is not to be the 'implementation enforcer' but rather to partner with teachers on their goals for student learning. What would you think about trying a coaching cycle with me to see how different this approach to coaching feels?"
A principal says, "I have some serious concerns about Mr. Seltzer's classroom management. With all of my other duties, I really need you to get in there and help him get on the right track."	"While I realize that you have some concerns, I wonder if we can take another approach to this. If I go in to work with Mr. Seltzer uninvited, I will be seen as a 'fixer,' which will undermine all the hard work we've done to create a positive culture around coaching. If you were to express your concerns to him and then suggest he seek out working with me for support, I think it will go a long way in keeping me away from the role of supervisor."

online resources 🔖   Available for download at **resources.corwin.com/EssentialGuideforSCCoaching**

Language for Connecting Coaching Cycles With Curriculum, Programs, and Classroom Management

IF I HEAR . . .	THEN I CAN USE THE FOLLOWING LANGUAGE . . .
"I don't have time for a whole coaching cycle. I just want you to show me how to use more technology in my classroom since our principal has been pushing for that."	"I'm happy to help you figure out how to use more technology. Tell me a bit more about what unit you have coming up. It would be great to partner on planning and teaching the actual unit, and we can think about what different tech tools will support student learning along the way."
"I'm not sure why we need to decide on a goal for students when the curriculum scope and sequence have everything mapped out for us. If you can just come in and model a couple of lessons for me, that would be great."	"The new reading curriculum definitely has a tight pacing guide. I think that if we look through the upcoming unit, we'll be able to pull out the big ideas that are tied to the standards. We can use that to help kids engage in the end goal, and we can work together to monitor their progress and make adjustments along the way. This will help us be more intentional as we learn the new curriculum together."
"Since we're working on a new behavior initiative, it seems like that should be the focus of what we work on together."	"There is definitely an expectation that we are all working on the new behavior program with students. But we still need to be helping them meet the standards as well. How about if we think of a goal for student learning and then figure out what behaviors from the program the kids will need to be successful in the learning? Then you and I can partner over the next several weeks to embed those things into our teaching to help your students meet the goal."

 Available for download at **resources.corwin.com/EssentialGuideforSCCoaching**

Language and Strategies for Measuring the Impact of Coaching

IF I HEAR OR NOTICE . . .	THEN I CAN SAY OR DO . . .
"I don't see the value in pre-assessing the students. I already know they don't know this material, so it would just be frustrating for them and a waste of time for me."	"Using pre- and post-assessment data that is descriptive and paints a picture of how students grew across a cycle gives us tangible evidence of the impact of our coaching work. For this reason, we don't simply give the end-of-unit test at the beginning of the unit. Rather, we try to get a more nuanced view of what the students already know in relation to the success criteria. The best way to do this is through an open-ended formative assessment."
"I feel like I know my students really well, and I can tell when they get something and when they don't. It feels like a lot of extra work to constantly have to be looking at all their work if it's just going to tell me what I already know."	"You really do have an amazing sense about your students. With so much happening each day, it can be really helpful to actually look at their work or anecdotal evidence so we are crystal clear about who is doing what. The key is to make sure we're formatively assessing so we can have a really accurate picture of where each student is and what they need next in their learning."
A coach expresses concern to her teammates that using the Results-Based Coaching Tool (RBCT) will feel too cumbersome to teachers and may make them avoid wanting to do coaching cycles.	A fellow coach can reply, "We need to help teachers see that documenting our work with the RBCT is not just about filling out a form but rather it's a way to help us stay focused on the goal for student learning throughout the coaching cycle and to measure student growth from beginning to end. Not every teacher may want to have the tool present in our daily collaboration, but if it's a shared online document, then they can choose whether to access it or not."

online resources 🔖 Available for download at **resources.corwin.com/EssentialGuideforSCCoaching**

Language and Strategies for Student-Centered Conversations

IF I HEAR OR NOTICE . . .	THEN I CAN SAY OR DO . . .
A grade-level team meets weekly to co-plan as part of their coaching cycle. Certain group members dominate the conversation. Their focus is on efficiency, and it seems like they don't want to take time for everyone to reflect as part of the learning process.	It's the facilitator's role to ensure that in collaborative conversations, groups are balanced and productive. In this case, the coach may lead the group to unpack the Seven Norms of Collaboration to uncover what it would look and feel like to put the norms into practice. At the end of each session, the group then uses the norms to reflect on the quality of their conversation and then set a goal for how they might continue to improve.
A coach and teacher are co-planning together. The teacher turns to the coach and says, "Since you know the curriculum, it would be great if you planned the lesson. Then you can just tell me what you want me to do."	The coach responds by saying, "I appreciate that, but you know your kids the best. How about if we start by doing a quick sort of your student work, and then we can sketch out the lesson together. This way, we'll both be able to think about the students and the curriculum at the same time. How does that sound?"
A teacher shares that the principal has been providing lots of feedback through the formal evaluation process. The teacher says, "I feel pretty good about it and don't really think I need to work with a coach."	The coach explains, "The feedback that you received as part of the evaluation process is completely different from what happens in Student-Centered Coaching. Rather than feeling like it is being done to you, coaching is a partnership that's about helping your students meet the goals you set for them."

online resources → Available for download at **resources.corwin.com/EssentialGuideforSCCoaching**

Language for Building a Culture That Supports Coaching

IF I HEAR . . .	THEN I CAN USE THE FOLLOWING LANGUAGE . . .
"I finally feel like I'm in a pretty good place with my teaching. I'm just not sure I want to take on all that's involved with coaching."	"Teaching is hard work, that's for sure. And it's tempting to want to maintain the status quo and catch our breath for a while. But if you're willing to embrace the messiness of learning together, I bet we can really take it to the next level with your students by building on all the great work you're already doing."
"I don't think I would feel comfortable with you telling our principal about the work you're doing in my class."	"Please know that my role is not to evaluate you or try to 'fix' you as a teacher. The idea is for us to work together to help your students learn. I would never speak with the principal about what you are or aren't doing in your classroom. Rather, I would share the different things we are trying and how your students are progressing toward meeting the goal we set for their learning."
"I have two students who have serious behavior issues and are derailing my whole class. Can you please take them to provide some targeted behavior intervention?"	"I think you'll want to take this concern to the intervention team. I'm not sure if you remember the presentation our principal and I gave during our last staff meeting, but she was explaining how coaching is going to look different this year from what we've had in the past. My role is not to provide interventions or just be a resource to teachers but to work with teachers in coaching cycles toward a goal for student learning."

online resources   Available for download at **resources.corwin.com/EssentialGuideforSCCoaching**

Strategies for Making Coaching Cycles Happen

IF I HEAR OR NOTICE . . .	THEN I CAN SAY OR DO . . .
"This is a new position for me, and I want to be seen as being useful to teachers, so I'm really willing to do whatever they ask of me."	Remember that a coach will be defined by how people see them spending their time. Therefore, it's important for me to get started with coaching cycles. Maybe there's a teacher or two who they can invite to participate in a cycle to practice and get some momentum.
"We just completed a time audit at the end of the first semester, and I'm barely getting into coaching cycles because there are so many other things taking up my time."	This is great data to share with the principal and building leadership team. Together, they can think creatively about ways to clear the coaches' plate to make more time to engage in cycles.
"It's the end of the first year with Student-Centered Coaching, and I worked with the same handful of teachers all year long. I couldn't seem to get others to engage."	This is a good time to reflect on the marketing that's been done throughout the year. How can you continue to help people understand what Student-Centered Coaching is and why it matters, especially the teachers who have yet to engage in coaching cycles?

online resources 🔍 Available for download at **resources.corwin.com/EssentialGuideforSCCoaching**

Language and Strategies for Hiring Effective Coaches

IF I HEAR OR NOTICE . . .	THEN I MIGHT THINK OR DO . . .
There are two candidates for a coaching position. One has worked at the school for twenty years. The other is from out of the district. Since coaching is built on relationships, it seems like a good idea to hire her. But the principal hesitates because it feels like teachers will perceive the hiring process as not being thorough or objective.	Formalizing (and de-personalizing) the hiring process is an important step. One option is to use the domains that are included on the Rubric for Student-Centered Coaching to make the expectations for the coaching role clear. It is also important to articulate that the rubric will also be used for evaluation processes. This moves the hiring process away from relationships and toward the practices and dispositions that are expected.
During an interview, a candidate for a high school coaching position says, "I see myself working with the math and science departments because I'm familiar with these subjects." When the principal hears this, he isn't sure how to respond because he doesn't want to hire a coach who lacks the confidence that is required to coach across content areas.	The principal may say, "What we are looking for is an understanding of pedagogy that stretches across content. We also value coaches who carry a learning disposition. That said, we are prepared to help you develop the skills that you will need as a coach." It's important to keep in mind that anyone who steps into the job must understand that we can't pick and choose who we work with. Rather, a coach must be confident enough to work with teachers across the faculty.
Thanks to support from the school board, the district posted job descriptions for twelve new coaching positions. So far, only four people have applied. The assistant superintendent knows that this is their chance to build an effective team of coaches but wonders why nobody wants the job.	Sometimes it's important to "go slow to go fast," and this may be one of those times. Doing some research to gather perceptions by teachers about coaching would help the district understand why teachers are not interested. We'd suggest to hold off on hiring any coaches until there is both a deeper candidate pool and a better understanding of the coaching role throughout the teaching ranks.

online resources ↘ Available for download at **resources.corwin.com/EssentialGuideforSCCoaching**

Resource B

Results-Based Coaching Tool

Coach Name:		Teacher Name(s):		
Dates of Coaching Cycle:		**Coaching Focus (Grade/Subject/Content):**		
Standards-Based Goal <u></u>What is the goal for student learning?	**Instructional Practice** What instructional practices will help students reach the goal?	**Instructional Coaching** What coaching practices were implemented during this coaching cycle?	**Teacher Learning** As a result of the coaching, what instructional practices are being used on a consistent basis?	**Student Learning** How did student learning increase as a result of the coaching cycle?
Students will . . . **Standard(s):** **Learning Targets:** I can:	**Teacher will . . .**	**Coach and teacher did . . .** (check all that apply) ☐ Goal setting ☐ Creating learning targets ☐ Analysis of student work ☐ Co-teaching ☐ Collecting student evidence during the class period ☐ Collaborative planning ☐ Shared learning to build knowledge of content and pedagogy	**Teacher is . . .**	**Students are . . .** **Student Learning** How did student learning increase as a result of the coaching cycle? **Post-Assessment Data:** ___ Emerging ___ Developing ___ Meeting ___ Exceeding ___ % of students were able to demonstrate proficiency of the learning targets

(Continued)

Baseline Data:	Other: _____	Follow-up for students who didn't reach the goal:
____ Emerging ____ Developing ____ Meeting ____ Exceeding ____ % of students were able to demonstrate proficiency of the learning targets		

(Continued)

(Continued)

TEACHER REFLECTIONS	COACH REFLECTIONS
How did the coaching cycle support the students' learning?	What coaching moves most supported the coaching cycle?
Were there any challenges or missed opportunities during the coaching cycle?	Were there any challenges or missed opportunities during the coaching cycle?
What are some next steps for your teaching as a result of the coaching cycle?	What are some next steps for your coaching as a result of the coaching cycle?

online resources

Available for download at **resources.corwin.com/EssentialGuideforSCCoaching**

Resource C

Success Criteria for
Building a Culture for Coaching

Members of the school community engage in behaviors that demonstrate collective efficacy.

Success Criteria:

- We avoid labeling students as low achieving. This means we are prepared to respectfully address incidences when our colleagues label students as low achieving.

- We see ourselves as having what it takes to be successful.

- We are not adversarial or competitive with one another.

- There is a platform for sharing successes, such as in faculty meetings, in a weekly bulletin, in grade-level meetings, in department meetings, etc.

- Certain teachers aren't favored over others. Rather, the successes of all teachers are shared.

Collaboration processes are rooted in student evidence.

Success Criteria:

- Collaboration, involving such groups as PLCs, data teams, departments, and attendees of grade-level meetings, includes analysis of student evidence or other forms of assessment data.

- Throughout day-to-day instruction, students engage in tasks that make their thinking visible. These are the formative assessments that are used during collaboration.

- Coaching cycles involve the continuous collection of student evidence.

- Student evidence is compared to the learning targets, or success criteria, to identify gaps in student performance and determine next steps for instruction.

School improvement is focused on one area of improvement at a time.

Success Criteria:

- There is a clear and well-understood focus of improvement.

- The learning focus is data driven and is captured in a well-organized school improvement plan.

- Teachers have a voice in determining the learning focus.

- Coaches support the learning focus through coaching cycles and other collaborative processes.

- Professional learning is differentiated for teachers based on their needs as well as the needs of their students.

 Available for download at **resources.corwin.com/EssentialGuidefor SCCoaching**

Resource D

Rubric for Student-Centered Coaching

Effective Coaches . . .

1. Understand and implement the core practices for Student-Centered Coaching.

2. Design systems and structures to engage teachers in coaching cycles.

3. Understand effective instruction and help teachers implement it.

4. Build trusting and respectful relationships with teachers.

5. Provide skilled facilitation during collaboration.

6. Maintain a learning stance.

7. Engage in reflective dialogue with teachers.

# 1: Understand and implement the core practices for Student-Centered Coaching.			
	Accomplished	*Developing*	*Novice*
The coach . . .	Consistently implements the core practices for Student-Centered Coaching. Thus, coaching leads to a measurable impact on instructional practice and student learning. The core practices are being implemented throughout the school community.	Is developing skill and confidence in using the core practices for Student-Centered Coaching. The core practices are being used with some teachers but not the full school community.	Is using practices for coaching that aren't student centered. This may include providing resources, holding teachers accountable for implementing programs, or serving as a quasi administrator.

(Continued)

(Continued)

Success Criteria	I can . . .
	• Organize most of my work to take place in coaching cycles.
	• Work with teachers to set standards-based goals for coaching cycles.
	• Work with teachers to unpack the goal into student-friendly learning targets.
	• Use student evidence when co-planning and co-teaching.
	• Co-plan lessons that integrate effective instructional practices.
	• Use co-teaching practices that build partnerships with teachers.
	• Measure the impact of coaching cycles on student and teacher learning.

2: Design systems and structures to engage teachers in coaching cycles.

	Accomplished	Developing	Novice
The coach . . .	Creates a well-organized system for managing coaching cycles that provides choice for how teachers can engage.	Offers some coaching cycles, but there is limited reach and/or effectiveness. Teachers aren't sure how or why they should engage in coaching cycles.	Spends very little time in coaching cycles and mostly serves as a resource to teachers.

Success Criteria	I can . . .
	• Set agreements with teachers before the coaching cycle begins.
	• Ensure that teachers have choice and ownership throughout a coaching cycle.
	• Maintain focus on the goal that was set by the teacher.
	• Provide opportunities to engage in coaching cycles throughout the school year.
	• Use logs and note-taking in a way that is transparent and includes the teacher.
	• Continually listen and respond to the needs of teachers.
	• Design and use a system for monitoring teacher participation in coaching cycles in order to engage others.

#3: Understand effective instruction, and help teachers implement it.

	Accomplished	Developing	Novice
The coach . . .	Has an extensive understanding of effective instructional practices across grades and subjects. The coach successfully supports others to implement these practices in their own classrooms.	Has some understanding of effective instructional practices but is learning how to transfer knowledge to the work of other teachers.	Either doesn't have a fully developed understanding of effective instructional practices and/or is unable to move teachers toward their own implementation.

Success Criteria	I can . . .
	• Articulate what effective practices are and why they matter to student learning.
	• Prioritize which practices to focus on at any given time.
	• Help move teachers forward in their learning while maintaining their ownership of the process.
	• Use student evidence when co-planning with teachers.
	• Co-plan with teachers in a way that intentionally builds effective practices into lessons.
	• Co-teach to implement effective instructional practice.
	• Continue to learn and grow in using effective instructional practices.

#4: Build trusting and respectful relationships with teachers.

	Accomplished	Developing	Novice
The coach . . .	Works effectively with all teachers due to specific measures he or she has taken to build trusting and professional relationships.	Is beginning to build trusting relationships with a broader array of teachers, including more challenging teachers.	Is able to build trusting relationships with a limited group of teachers.
Success Criteria	I can . . .		

- Build collegial relationships that are trusting and respectful.
- Use a respectful tone throughout my coaching conversations.
- Avoid being a "teller" but rather be a "co-constructor" of learning.
- Avoid focusing on weaknesses but rather build on strengths.
- Ask open-ended questions.
- Set a tone that "we are all learners."

#5: Provide skilled facilitation during collaboration.

	Accomplished	Developing	Novice
The coach . . .	Understands which facilitation processes to employ at any given time. The coach is a skilled facilitator and, as a result, both small and large groups function in a highly productive manner on a consistent basis.	Is working to expand the repertoire of facilitation techniques used in small- and large-group sessions. Groups are beginning to function at a more productive level.	Employs a limited set of facilitation processes. Small- and/or large-group facilitation are not productive on a consistent basis.

(Continued)

(Continued)

Success Criteria	I can . . .
	• Use strategies for facilitation to guide group learning.
	• Use (or create) protocols that contribute to the learning of the group.
	• Anchor conversations in student work.
	• Encourage teacher choice and ownership during collaboration.
	• Listen and respond in a way that honors the group.
	• Use the Seven Norms of Collaborative Work to support teachers to reflect as learners.
	• Manage interactions between peers in a collegial way.
	• Respectfully intervene if collegial interactions are toxic or harmful.

#6: Maintain a learning stance

	Accomplished	Developing	Novice
The coach . . .	Consistently seeks new experiences and opportunities for learning rather than taking the stance of an "expert."	Takes advantage of some opportunities for new learning and is becoming more comfortable regarding taking the stance of "co-learner" with teachers.	Does not take advantage of opportunities for new learning on a consistent basis and does not take the stance of "co-learner" with teachers.

Success Criteria	I can . . .
	• Demonstrate that I am a learner inside and outside of school.
	• Take risks that are inherent to learning.
	• Share how my thinking evolves based on the input of others.
	• Build collegial relationships based on my own learning.
	• Establish a trusting and respectful tone throughout my coaching conversations.
	• Create systems for teachers to share ideas and resources with one another.

#7: Engage in reflective dialogue with teachers

	Accomplished	Developing	Novice
The coach . . .	Encourages reflective dialogue by asking open-ended questions, probing, and using paraphrasing techniques rather than simply giving the teacher answers.	Is beginning to use strategies such as asking open-ended questions, probing, and paraphrasing techniques to encourage reflective dialogue among teachers.	Does not use conversational approaches that encourage reflective dialogue among teachers.

Success Criteria	I can . . .
	• Use student work as a means of encouraging reflection.
	• Listen (avoid talking too much or making too many suggestions that may overwhelm teachers).
	• Take a strengths-based approach to conversations.
	• Paraphrase to honor and/or clarify the thoughts of others.
	• Ask probing questions that I don't know the answer to.
	• Maintain an open mind as the teachers' learning progresses.

online resources ↘ Available for download at **resources.corwin.com/EssentialGuideforSCCoaching**

Resource E

Coaching Lab Overview

Overview

- Coaching labs are an opportunity to engage in job-embedded professional development as a coaching team. The labs are structured to include an observation of a coach in action and then a debrief to unpack implications and points of learning that relate to our work with teachers. A prebrief also provides time for the coach to set the focus and share tools and strategies that have been used.

- Coaching labs are not designed to model coaching. Rather, they are a chance to stretch our thinking as coaches. Typically, coaching lab hosts are open and reflective, and they are willing to share their practice and challenges with others. The host selects the focus for the observation and whether or not it will include a lesson. The facilitator works with the host to ensure that she or he feels prepared.

Things to Consider

- Coaching lab hosts aren't experts; they are learners. We are not observing with the purpose of "learning from the master." We are observing to expand our thinking, generate questions, and develop a view of what Student-Centered Coaching looks like in our schools.

- Coaching labs are limited to ten participants.

- Coaching labs are authentic examples of our work; we like to avoid dog and pony shows.

- Coaching labs adhere to a protocol and norms for observation.

Planning for Coaching Labs

- A lab host is determined, and then the lab host identifies the teacher(s) who will participate.

- The lab host determines the focus of the coaching lab.

- The facilitator and lab host plan the focus and schedule in a planning call.

- The teacher only participates in the observation portions of the coaching lab. She or he doesn't attend the prebrief or debrief.

Coaching Lab Protocol

Goal for the Coaching Cycle:	
Learning Target(s) for the Lesson:	
Prebrief (30–45 minutes)	The facilitator introduces the protocol and shares the norms for the observation. The coach provides background about the coaching work that is taking place with the teacher or team of teachers. This includes sharing the learning target(s) and plan for the lesson. The coach may also choose to share tools, logs, and artifacts that have been used to organize the coaching work. Participants are invited to ask clarifying questions. **Observation Norms for Coaching Labs** • Come with a positive attitude, and be a learner. We are not here to critique or give feedback to the coach or teacher. • Avoid side conversations. Please do not speak to students unless it has been an established part of the process. • Get close to the action by collecting student evidence during the lesson. A note catcher will be provided for this purpose. • Be ready to think through the entire process. This includes the prebrief, observation, and debrief. Participants are expected to be a part of the full process, rather than popping into certain portions. Note: The teacher does not attend the prebrief.

Observe the Co-Teaching Session (30–45 minutes)	Participants observe the teacher and coach as they work together in the classroom. Observers practice noticing and naming during this part of the process. The facilitator provides a note catcher for this purpose.
Observe the Co-Planning Session (30 minutes)	Participants observe as the teacher and coach co-plan using the student evidence that was gathered during the lesson. While observing, participants take notes to capture the coaching moves and language that are used.
Debrief the Coaching (60 minutes)	Participants debrief in the following rounds. During the first three rounds the lab host is a silent observer. Then the host joins in after Round 3 to answer questions and share thinking. **Round 1: What happened?** • Participants take turns describing what they noticed during either part of the observation. The focus may be on the student learning, coaching moves, coaching language, etc. Use objective language, such as: "I saw," "I heard," "I noticed." **Round 2: What does it mean?** • Participants share implications for student and teacher learning that surfaced as a result of the observation. A possible stem is "Because . . . then . . ." **Round 3: What do I wonder?** • Participants share questions that were elicited as a result of the observation. These can be about either the observation itself or something related to their own coaching practice. The facilitator collects the questions that are then addressed by the coach. **Round 4: What are my next steps?** • Participants share a next step for their own learning.

online resources — Available for download at **resources.corwin.com/EssentialGuideforSCCoaching**

References

Aguilar, E. (2013). *The art of coaching*. San Francisco, CA: John Wiley.

Almarode, J., & Vandas, K. (2018). *Clarity for learning*. Thousand Oaks, CA: Corwin.

Amabile, T., & Kramer, S. J. (2011). *The power of small wins*. Cambridge, MA: Harvard Business Journal. Retrieved from https://hbr.org/2011/05/the-power-of-small-wins

Barth, R. (2007). *Educational leadership*. San Francisco, CA: Jossey-Bass.

Black, P., & Wiliam, D. (1998). Inside the black box: Raising standards through classroom assessment. *Phi Delta Kappan, 80*(2), 139–144, 146–148.

Bryk, A., & Schneider, B. (2003). Trust in schools: A core resource for school reform. *Educational Leadership, 60*(6), 40–45.

Buckingham, M., & Goodall, A. (2019, March–April). The feedback fallacy. *Harvard Business Review*. Retrieved from https://hbr.org/2019/03/the-feedback-fallacy

Cheliotes, L. G., & Reilly, M. F. (2010). *Coaching conversations: One conversation at a time*. Thousand Oaks, CA: Corwin.

Covey, S. R. (2004). *The 7 habits of highly effective people: Powerful lessons in personal change*. New York, NY: Simon & Schuster.

Darling-Hammond, L., Hyler, M. E., & Gardner, M. (2017). *Effective teacher professional development*. Palo Alto, CA: Learning Policy Institute.

Donohoo, J. (2017). *Collective efficacy*. Thousand Oaks, CA: Corwin.

Evans, R. (1996). *The human side of school change*. San Francisco, CA: Jossey-Bass.

Fullan, M. (2001). *Leading in a culture of change*. San Francisco, CA: Jossey-Bass.

Garmston, R. J., & Wellman, B. M. (2016). *The adaptive school: A sourcebook for developing collaborative groups*. Lanham, MD: Rowman & Littlefield.

Gladwell, M. (2008). *Outliers: The story of success*. New York, NY: Back Bay Books.

Guskey, T. (1995). *Professional development in education*. New York, NY: Teachers College Press.

Guskey, T. (2000). *Evaluating professional development*. Thousand Oaks, CA: Corwin.

Guskey, T., & McTighe, J. (2016). Pre-assessment: Promises and cautions. *Educational Leadership, 73*(7), 38–43.

Hattie, J. (2009). *Visible learning: A synthesis of over 800 meta-analyses relating to achievement*. New York, NY: Routledge.

Hattie, J. (2012). *Visible learning for teachers: Maximizing impact on learning*. Thousand Oaks, CA: Corwin.

Hattie, J. (2019, June). Visible learning™: 250+ influences on student achievement. Retrieved from https://us.corwin.com/sites/default/files/250_ influences_chart_june_2019.pdf

Hattie, J., & Zierer, K. (2018). *10 mindframes for visible learning*. New York, NY: Routledge.

Heineke, S., & Polnick, B. (2013). Pave the way for coaches: Principal's actions are key to shaping roles and relationships. *Learning Forward, 34*(3), 48–51.

McDonald, J. (2017). Tuning protocol. *School Reform Initiative*. Retrieved from https://www.schoolreforminitiative.org/download/tuning-protocol

McTighe, J., & Wiggins, G. (2012). *Understanding by design white paper*. Alexandria, VA: ASCD. Retrieved from https://www.ascd.org/ASCD/pdf/site ASCD/publications/UbD_WhitePaper0312.pdf

Popham, J. (2008). *Transformative assessment*. Alexandria, VA: ASCD.

Schmoker, M. (2019). Embrace the power of less. *Educational Leadership, 76*(6), 24–29.

Sinek, S. (2009). *Start with the why—How great leaders inspire action*. TedXPugetSound. Retrieved from https://www.ted.com/talks/simon_sinek_ how_great_leaders_inspire_action

SoulPancake & Edutopia. (2014, May 3). *If I knew then: A letter to me on my first day teaching* [Video file]. Retrieved from https://www.youtube.com/ watch?v=miPYLJI247g

Stenberg, A. (2015). *What is the Rule of Seven? And how will it improve your marketing?* Retrieved from https://www.thebabyboomerentrepreneur .com/258/what-is-the-rule-of-seven-and-how-will-it-improve-your-marketing

Sweeney, D. (2003). *Learning along the way.* Portsmouth, NH: Stenhouse.

Sweeney, D. (2011). *Student-centered coaching: A guide for K–8 coaches and principals.* Thousand Oaks, CA: Corwin.

Sweeney, D. (2013). *Student-centered coaching at the secondary level.* Thousand Oaks, CA: Corwin.

Sweeney, D., & Harris, L. (2017). *Student-centered coaching: The moves.* Thousand Oaks, CA: Corwin.

Sweeney, D., & Mausbach, A. (2018). *Leading student-centered coaching: Building principal and coach partnerships.* Thousand Oaks, CA: Corwin.

Tschannen-Moran, M. (2004). *Trust matters: Leadership for successful schools.* San Francisco, CA: Jossey-Bass.

Wiggins, G., & McTighe, J. (2005). *Understanding by design* (2nd ed.). Alexandria, VA: ASCD.

Index